A Clinician's Guide to Pathological Ambivalence

How to Be on Your Client's Side Without Taking a Side

Linda Paulk Buchanan, PhD

Contents

Preface

As a therapist, you undoubtedly have had the experience of working with a patient who spends a lot of money and time coming to therapy, only to avoid doing what you suggest. These patients are often labeled *resistant*, *oppositional*, or *borderline*, in part because of the frustration they create in those who want to help them. Therapists concurrently may label themselves as ineffective or unskilled while working with these patients. When dealing with someone with *pathological ambivalence*, such labels are unnecessary and generally inaccurate. Instead, the client and therapist will benefit by using specific strategies to identify, manage, and resolve their ambivalence.

After working for 30 years with people with eating disorders (the past 25 years at the Atlanta Center for Eating Disorders, a partial hospitalization and intensive outpatient program I founded), I have learned a great deal about working with treatment-resistant or ambivalent patients. Maybe more than in any other client population, ambivalence among those with eating disorders can be pathological. The very thing that makes them believe they can manage their problems in life actually is *life-threatening*. While the patients may be seeking help, they often feel as if they are being forced to give up behaviors that provide them, albeit irrationally, with a sense of safety and ability to cope with life.

These patients engage in meal groups at our center. It is all too common to get into power struggles in this context while trying to get them to eat. One evening, as we sat together, I observed one member struggling. With every bite she took, I could see the distress etched in the sharp contours of her face. My conversation with her went like this: "Lilly, you seem to be debating and agonizing over every single bite, asking yourself whether you should put it in your mouth." She smiled sadly and nodded, apparently surprised that I understood her internal experience and recognizing how trapped she felt. I sighed with an expression of pained empathy on my face and said, "This must be terrible," adding, "I hate to see you suffer so much. If the batteries hadn't died in my magic wand, I would wave it right now and take away some of your suffering." The use of humor helped her know that I wasn't judging her. Similarly, referring to the magic wand was a metaphor for communicating to her that I knew I didn't have the power to *make* her want to eat.

I went on to suggest that she take a portion of the meal that she knew she was going to eat and go ahead and make an absolute decision. This way, she wouldn't have to re-decide with every bite. I explained to Lilly that my hope was to decrease her suffering so that she would only have to debate with herself two or three times during the meal. The conversation helped her think about how she was causing herself to suffer so much. Lilly later told me that it had been a turning point in her recovery.

After 3 decades of working with treatment-resistant patients, I determined that to successfully treat people with eating disorders (Schaffner & Buchanan, 2008, 2010), a theory for working with extreme ambivalence was necessary. I came up with the concept of *pathological ambivalence* to explain the underlying mechanisms of "resistance" and to inform the strategic interventions best used with this population. Although the patients I spend the most time with have eating disorders, this theory applies to people with a multitude of diagnoses. The theory encompasses why we experience ambivalence, the factors that make some people more susceptible than others to developing pathological ambivalence, and the importance of forming our narrative to guide us through life.

The theory posits that pathological ambivalence will occur when certain factors converge during a person's development and create a conflict in core needs. This is not so-called normal ambivalence, such as choosing whether to go out to dinner or stay home. Pathological ambivalence occurs when what has been learned about core needs is in conflict with the necessity of having the core needs met. The narratives that are then developed are ruled by these conflicting needs. For example, the universal core needs of love and safety can be in conflict when a person has learned that it seems safer never to expect to be loved. However, the core need for love doesn't disappear, resulting in an inability to attempt to meet the needs for love and safety simultaneously.

This conflict of needs can lead to life-crippling dilemmas. Similarly in psychotherapy, the alternating expression of these needs results in behavior often labeled as resistant, such as therapy-interfering behaviors, power struggles, and even suicidal ideation.

A guide to dealing with pathological ambivalence is necessary to enable the clinician to quickly identify when core needs are in conflict, to help the patient become aware of the associated maladaptive narratives that have developed as a result of these conflicts, and to develop treatment strategies for harnessing and resolving the ambivalence. Dealing directly with this ambivalence is the primary therapeutic strategy to facilitate change. Without specific direction and support, it can take therapists years to build the skills necessary for dealing with clients' resistance and ambivalence. In this book, I provide case examples of how the expression of pathological ambivalence affects therapy and guide the reader in ways to sidestep common therapist pitfalls while also helping clients understand their ambivalence and rewrite their early narratives.

The subtitle of the book, *How to Be on Your Client's Side Without Taking a Side*, illuminates the natural tendency of therapists to get caught, so to speak, between the two sides of the patient's dilemma. Taking a side can occur when a therapist aligns with one side of the patient's ambivalence (usually the side desiring change) leaving the patient to respond from the side that fears change. This split occurs within the patient. Therefore, this book focuses on multiple strategies that enable the therapist to remain neutral while facilitating change.

Taking a side can also occur between the patient and others in the patient's interpersonal system. This subtitle came to me as I was supervising staff and students who were so focused on listening to and validating their clients that they naturally wanted to believe everything they were told. They often sided *with* the patient, even when the patient's perspective was distorted or was a projection of false narratives. Such an endeavor, although well meaning, often leaves the patient stuck in personal narratives or beliefs that may be ruining her life.

I would hear staff talking about how bad this person's father was or how horrible that person's boss was. I found myself jokingly asking the students if they actually had met the person to whom the patient was referring. I interjected "allegedly" when they would share stories about the patient or his past that involved another person. If the patients' perspectives were always accurate, they probably wouldn't need to be in therapy. Supervision often became primarily about teaching students how to be *on* their client's side without *taking* a side. Valuable therapy time can be wasted chasing the client down well-worn paths rather than empowering him to shift his thinking or perspective to be more effective. This issue is difficult for many therapists to acknowledge, and it is even more difficult to recognize when it is happening. My goal in writing this book is to help readers recognize that although we naturally take our clients' side, we also need skills to determine when this is not in their best interest.

For instance, in our clinic, clients often came to therapy with stories about what others did *to* them. However, during the course of therapy, they often would begin to complain about similar things happening at our center, such as feeling as if staff liked other patients more, or that we didn't really care, or that the patient had been verbally abused by another group member who was gently giving feedback. Now *we* were experiencing the "other side of the story" as *we* became the objects of their projections. At that point, we often found ourselves *siding against* the client. For example, we might start talking about how this client wasn't responding because she had problems with trust, etc. Common therapeutic mistakes that occur when dealing with ambivalence include blaming the patient, engaging in power struggles, and attempting to change the client's mind rather than facilitate her ability to resolve ambivalence.

These mistakes happen when the therapist has not fully assessed early client scripts that are fueling ambivalence or identified how those scripts affect the client's feelings, behaviors, and interpersonal relationships. This results in what I call "falling into the split." Other common pitfalls discussed in this book include dealing with only one side of the dilemma at a time, failing to recognize when a projection is operating, prematurely challenging a script, personalizing the resistance, engaging in power struggles, taking on the client's hopelessness, and taking on too much or too little responsibility for the client's success.

The book is divided into three parts. In the first part, "Understanding Ambivalence as Resistance to Change," I focus on defining and describing pathological ambivalence and present a model for understanding how it is developed and maintained in a person's life.

I review early theorists' writings about resistance, focusing on those whose ideas inform the strategies outlined later in Part III. Finally, I describe factors involved in developing pathological ambivalence, such as the highly sensitive person, brain factors, and attachment styles.

Part II, "Developing a Dialectical Perspective for Recognizing Pathological Ambivalence," introduces a dialectical therapeutic frame for addressing pathological ambivalence while exploring its common manifestations, such as power struggles, indirect communication, projection, splitting, avoidance, and denial, so that it quickly can be identified in the therapeutic process. In this section, I also describe common therapeutic pitfalls to avoid when working with people with pathological ambivalence and how to deal with the projection of the ambivalence or narrative.

I devote Part III, "Treatment Strategies for Pathological Ambivalence," to techniques for working with the various forms of pathological ambivalence, primarily through case examples. Beginning with a description of issues related to assessment and education specific to this population. I then recommend strategies, grouped by primary therapeutic goal, to help the therapist address each side of the dilemma. One collection of strategies is aimed at decreasing the natural tendency to maintain the status quo of previously held beliefs (such as, "I'm not lovable") and at enabling the patient to see the impossible state of her ambivalence. Another section focuses on integrating the two sides of the dilemma by identifying the truths and fallacies, so that the ambivalence can be resolved and change enabled. The final set of strategies is devoted to rewriting the early narrative into a more functional belief set or story about oneself and the world. I use a variety of techniques from many theoretical orientations, including gestalt, cognitive-behavioral, and psychodynamic, and from techniques informed by narrative therapy, motivational interviewing, and acceptance and commitment therapy.

As mentioned, this book offers an overview of historical and theoretical perspectives on resistance. It expands on concepts written in other books related to resistance, such as *Ambivalence in Psychotherapy: Facilitating Readiness to Change*, by Engle and Arkowitz (2006). My goal is to condense, integrate, and simplify many theories and strategies related to resistance in an effort to present the rich history of practice and research that undergird the concepts presented here. Thus, this book can be used as a textbook to accelerate the learning process for beginning therapists but also as a useful reference tool for therapists with years of experience. Regardless of theoretical orientation, therapists will be able to relate to the concepts and strategies presented and can begin using those they already understand specifically to address resistance.

I will alternately refer to the person in therapy as *client* or *patient* and as *he, she, him,* or *her.* The case examples I share are related from memory in a fashion that captures the point being made or the skill being taught. The names and any identifying characteristics of current or former clients have been changed to protect their privacy.

Every concept included in this book has been influenced by something that I've been taught or read. I have used my own terms for a few concepts (see *idling emotion* and *burnt food syndrome*) but even these refer to identifiable human experiences that probably have gone by any number of names. My hope is that by organizing these concepts and strategies related to ambivalence and sharing stories about my clients, this book will deepen your understanding and enjoyment of working with your clients and patients, especially when they seem to be resistant to your efforts.

Acknowledgments

First and foremost, I must acknowledge the courageous and dedicated patients who have trusted me with their stories. Every person represented in this book has captured a place in my heart and will remain there forever. It is an awesome privilege to be allowed to walk for a time in the story of someone's life and to play some small part in easing his or her burden.

I also must thank my husband and two sons, who have encouraged me along the way with this book. My husband, Bill Buchanan, PhD, also a psychologist, supports me in all my endeavors. At any moment when I was writing, I could ask him to come and read a passage and give me feedback. This was very loving and invaluable to me.

I thank my team at the Atlanta Center for Eating Disorders who have helped me develop my teaching skills and who have been adamant about the need for this type of book to be available to clinicians. They have read various versions during this process and given me helpful advice when something wasn't clear.

I'd like to thank my friend and fellow Zumba dancer, Uli Sotunde, who was writing her first book as I was writing this one. Her support and ideas along the way helped take a project that can be very isolating into the interpersonal realm in a fun way.

Big thanks goes to my high school English teacher, Mr. Hines. He inspired a love and a measure of skill for writing. I remember working very hard all those years ago to learn the mechanics of writing, and the effort resulted in a love for putting concepts on paper.

I also thank my colleague friends, Lisa Tallant, Ronee Griffith, and Anja Schoeke, who volunteered to read an early draft and who helped shape some of the concepts and organization of this book. These therapists have much talent and commitment. Their feedback was invaluable.

I definitely do not thank my cat, Indy, who had to be on my lap during most of the typing of this book and slowed that process immeasurably.

Finally, I'd like to thank my dad, who has always been one of my biggest fans as well as an inspiration. Once, when he was objecting to my choice in a boyfriend, I said, "But, Dad, to know him is to love him." He responded with a statement that, though not original, had a great impact on me. He said, "Yes, Linda, to know anyone is to love them," which he wryly followed up with, "but that doesn't mean that I want them dating my daughter!" To know *anyone* is to love them—as in understanding the source of their ambivalence even when they are acting completely resistant or unlovable. This is certainly true of all the individuals with whom I've partnered in the change process and, thus, the motivation behind writing this book.

Part I

Understanding Resistance as Ambivalence to Change

Chapter 1: What Is So Difficult About Change?

Resistance Conceptualized as Ambivalence

I've been conducting therapy for more than 30 years. When I encountered resistance early in my career, I would feel frustrated and eager to get past the resistance so that we could get on with the *real* therapy. Thanks, however, to the specific experiences I had in my training and career, I discovered that lack of change often occurs when different parts in a system (whether internal or interpersonal) have differing wishes or needs that are not being integrated. All people have parts, and different parts of the same person can have different needs or wishes, such as needing companionship but fearing rejection. When resistance is encountered in psychotherapy, it is usually because either the client or therapist (or both) doesn't realize that the resistance is actually caused by ambivalence. Thus, when a therapist takes a side (presumably the part that wants to change in a healthy direction), the client is likely to voice the other side, resulting in what looks like resistance. Therefore, the therapist must learn how to be *on* the client's side without *taking* a side.

Although ambivalence is a normal human experience, it is considered to be pathological when it interferes with the client's ability to have a reasonably satisfying life and progress in therapy.

Ambivalence Conceptualized as the Key to Change

As so many therapists know (but like me, may have trouble remembering at times), the real therapy is working with the ambivalence. The resistance tells us where the pain is, and therefore on what the therapy must focus. Here are some key points to remember when feeling frustrated about resistance and ambivalence:

- If the patient weren't resistant or ambivalent, he probably wouldn't need you; one of many self-help books would do the trick.
- Most people naturally feel some resistance to change.
- Resistance shows us where the pain is.
- Resistance may be indicative of the interpersonal developmental level of the patient.
- Resistance exists in part on a physiological level due to neurological development.
- The very thing that brings clients to therapy is the thing that they are most afraid to change.
- Resistance may be a reaction to a therapist who is trying too hard to help.

When a therapist forgets that dealing with resistance is actually the *meat* of the therapy, he or she is probably operating from the assumption that the patient is being resistant without good reason, and thus being irrational. Or, as the therapist, we often personalize the resistance by feeling that the patient is doing something *to* us, such as vying for power, trying to frustrate us, or rejecting us. These feelings can lead to countertransference issues, such as becoming frustrated, working too hard to win over the patient, or even rejecting the patient.

Ambivalence Conceptualized as Normal

If we recognize that we all feel resistant or ambivalent when it comes to change, we are more empowered to understand our clients' ambivalence. Ambivalence to change occurs because whatever needs to change developed naturally at some point. Although ambivalence is normal, many people will realize why they're ambivalent and move on, resolving their internal conflicts.

Procrastination is a common example of how we all go through this process at times. For example, suppose "Jane" is procrastinating on scheduling a routine medical appointment. On the one hand, she wants to take care of her health; on the other hand, a few of her friends have recently had scary diagnoses. If she pauses to explore the source of her procrastination, she may discover her ambivalence, weigh the pros and cons (teasing apart her ambivalence), and decide to make the appointment (resolving the resistance through choice). Recognizing that she is ambivalent, Jane reassures herself that she only needs to take one step at a time and will have the support she needs if she should get bad news (reintegrating the ambivalence with new thoughts).

Ambivalence Toward Change Is Related to Brain Functioning

Ambivalence is normal, and much of one's ambivalence toward change can be attributed to various aspects of brain functioning. Every time we repeat a thought, feeling, or behavior, the neuropathway of that experience is strengthened. As described in *Mindsight*, the seminal book by Daniel Siegel (2011), our brain naturally functions to *develop associations* as a way of learning and saving energy: "What wires together fires together" (p. 40). For instance, when you get into your car, you can start driving with no thought about where the key goes and how to move out of park into drive. Your brain has taken several distinct experiences and formed a continuous and smooth habit that is mostly unconscious. But try getting into someone else's car for the first time, and it is awkward. Thus, change can be like trying to write with your nondominant hand: awkward and inefficient at first, but it can improve with practice. Due to many factors I describe later in the book, there are numerous forces within us that work against change.

Most learned associations are adaptive at the time in which they were formed, but what brings people to therapy is when the associations are no longer adaptive to their *current* circumstances or if their interpretations were made at a time when the person was too young to evaluate or interpret their associations or assumptions accurately. For example, a child might associate sickness with love if she received more attention and love when she was sick. This could lead to a chronic and possibly subconscious pattern of needing to be sick to believe that people care about her. As Dr. Victor Frankl (1946/2006), a Dachau concentration camp survivor, famously wrote in his book *Man's Search for Meaning*, "An abnormal reaction to an abnormal situation is normal behavior" (p. 32).

Another factor related to the difficulty to change is that under intense arousal, the associations are greatly strengthened. Such learning is imprinted immediately into the nervous system and thus doesn't require the repetition needed for most learning (e.g., times tables). The idea that emotional arousal influences memory is nothing new; in 1620, Francis Bacon (1620/2000) wrote about memory as being assisted by passion in that lasting impressions were influenced by the level of emotion associated with them. For instance, in the case of a trauma, the experience is so intense and the imprinting so efficient that something minimally or tangentially related to the trauma, such as an odor, can trigger the brain to fire in such a way that one reexperiences the entire event as if it were happening in the current moment (Cahill & Alkire, 2003; Liu, Graham, & Zorawski, 2008; McGaugh, 2015; Michael, Ehlers, & Halligan, 2005).

Furthermore, studies have shown that learning is more efficient when paired with negative emotion (Rozin & Royzman, 2001). This may have survival value. For example, suppose you live in the wild, and one day you are chased by a bear near a running stream. Your brain quickly and efficiently records all aspects of the dangerous situation, so that at first sign of a similar danger, you will be able to flee without having to consciously think about it. However, that experience can be overgeneralized, such that if you hear running water from a stream that has no bears living nearby, you may become very anxious and eventually have trouble leaving your hut, for fear of meeting a bear—unless you intentionally reevaluate your memory to determine if every stream should be feared and avoided.

Another brain factor that affects resistance is the neural *connectivity* between parts of the brain. The connections between emotional regions of the brain to the areas responsible for planning may not have sufficient connectivity, so that when the person is processing emotional stimuli, it might be harder to think about how best to act on the emotion (Banks, Kamryn, Angstadt, Pradeep, & Phan, 2007). Under these conditions, it can be challenging to monitor one's thoughts, senses, emotions, and actions, resulting in impulsivity or a diminished ability to shift mental states (Siegel, 2011). Additionally, when a person is experiencing a certain level of arousal, the prefrontal lobes go *off-line*, and the brain relies more on instinct and limbic functioning, focusing only on how to attend to a real or imagined extreme threat. There is no time to be mindful, observing and describing what is happening, followed by choosing an effective way to participate in the moment. The person either runs or fights or freezes. People who have experienced periods of high or chronic stress during childhood may have overused this part of their brain and may habitually return to fight, flight, or freeze, even when the stress is less extreme. Similarly, people who are highly sensitive (see Chapter 2 for a thorough discussion) in general overuse this part of the brain and therefore have greater difficulty using their prefrontal lobes to manage the stress. The good news is that even if a person's brain has less connectivity, this condition can be improved by forming new neural pathways between these areas through mindful awareness.

In summary, we see that ambivalence can be normal and adaptive, *or* a result of dysfunction. Once the brain has learned something, it is difficult to unlearn. This can result in resistance to change, experienced as ambivalence. It's a normal human condition. Just consider all the phrases we have for ambivalence: Of two minds, I'm torn, it's a dilemma, the jury's still out, waffling, it's debatable, vacillating, wavering, having a foot in both camps, hem and haw, it's a quandary, sitting on the fence, in limbo, wishy-washy. I love the scenes from *Fiddler on the Roof* where Tevye expresses his ambivalence while talking with God by saying "on the one hand ... but on the other hand ...." In one famous scene, he says it about six times (of course we don't have that many hands). In frustration at one point he yells, "No! There is no other hand!" This endearing character demonstrates the humanness of ambivalence as well as ways to work through it. Sometimes and for some people, however, this is very difficult to do.

The Themes of Pathological Ambivalence

Although we all experience ambivalence, it can become pathological in nature. As a student first being introduced to theoretical perspectives, I became fascinated by what I perceived were common threads among seemingly opposite theories regarding the nature of human personality and the nature of behavior change. I became interested in the subject of resistance and looked closely at the ways in which the early and more recent theorists defined resistance. Two primary themes emerged.

All People Have Parts

In what is referred to as the *multiplicity of human personality*, we all have parts. This explains how a person can want or need opposing things at the same time and therefore experience ambivalence. Furthermore, awareness of these parts and the level of integration we experience among them is affected by both the amount of stress we have endured as well as how reactive we are physiologically to stress. Thus we are affected by both learning and genetics in our susceptibility to developing pathological ambivalence.

In formulating my theory of pathological ambivalence, I was inspired by two sets of experiences that shaped my understanding of parts and systems. First, in my studies of family therapy in my doctoral program, I learned that family systems have parts with differing wants or needs. Those families that function well comprise many distinct parts working together as an integrated whole. On the other hand, dysfunctional families have splits, triangles, coalitions, and unhealthy hierarchies, which can undermine the healthy functioning of each part. My background in helping families resolve their differences informed my understanding of working with resistant or challenging clients. It became clear to me that taking a side was almost never the way to facilitate change with couples or families or even in individual therapy.

Second, during the process of working with several clients who were diagnosed with multiple personality disorder (now referred to as dissociative identity disorder, or DID), I noticed that they improved more rapidly by focusing on integrating parts through what is known as the host personality. When the therapy was too heavily focused on the various parts of the system, the client often became worse or more disintegrated. But multiplicity is not limited to people with DID. We all have parts—a child part, a wise adult part, a professional part, for example, all of which can be quite distinct from each other and have differing wants or needs. When you say to yourself, "I want to be fit, but I don't want to exercise," you are expressing differing needs from different parts of yourself.

All People Develop Narratives

Another main concept that has been incorporated into my theory of pathological ambivalences is that we all create schemas and narratives that guide us through life. These schemas may contain varying degrees of objective reality, which are then projected onto current situations. I was heavily influenced in my understanding of human behavior by Alfred Adler's 1964, 1928/2014) concepts—specifically that of the "Story of My Life." I even conducted research on the construct of early recollections as a treatment strategy to understand the themes that are prevalent in a client's story.

Pathological Ambivalence Defined

We've established that everyone is ambivalent about change to some extent, but not everyone develops *pathological ambivalence*. The *American Heritage Dictionary* (2011a, 2011b) defines *ambivalence* as (1) the co-existence of opposing attitudes or feelings, such as love and hate, toward a person, object, or idea and (2) the uncertainty as to which course to follow. *Pathology* is defined as (1) the scientific study of the nature of disease and its causes, processes, development and consequences and (2) departure or deviation from a normal, or efficient condition.

Ambivalence is considered pathological when it results in dysfunction in living, depression, disabling anxiety, and dysfunctional relationships. When pathological ambivalence is operating, a person's self-talk includes statements such as,

> *No one will care for my needs, but I secretly, maybe even unconsciously, crave the experience of being taken care of. Therefore, I need to act in a way that will get you to take care of me. However, I can't believe that you will care for my needs regardless of what you do, so I need to act in a way that shows that I don't care or need you.*

Sounds confusing, right? It is, and it's a life-crippling dilemma. The flowchart in Figure 1.1 depicts how this dilemma is maintained. Notice how the actions are mutually exclusive, yet coexist.

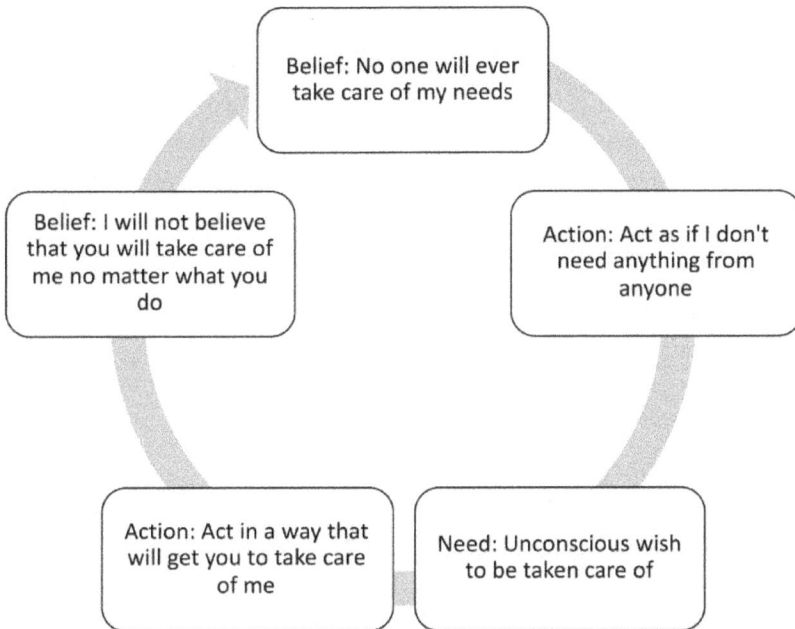

Belief: No one will ever take care of my needs

Action: Act as if I don't need anything from anyone

Need: Unconscious wish to be taken care of

Action: Act in a way that will get you to take care of me

Belief: I will not believe that you will take care of me no matter what you do

Figure 1.1 Dialectical beliefs flowchart. (Created by Linda Buchanan.)

Ambivalence is part of the remarkable complexity of being human in that we are capable of having many perspectives and feelings about the same event. Pathological ambivalence can take many forms, and, like most human experience or characteristics, it exists on a continuum from neurotic to extreme ambivalence; the latter can result in a complete break with reality. When reading through the levels of ambivalence described in the following paragraphs, keep in mind that there is always interplay between the physiology of the sensitive person and the hardship in the environment, such that different people in the same environment can develop different levels of ambivalence. That's why one sibling may be affected differently from another by similar experiences in a family unit. Additionally, just as there is a continuum in severity among the levels, there is a continuum of severity within each level, as well.

Neurotic Ambivalence

Neurotic ambivalence is the level most often seen in psychotherapy. It is characterized by difficulty making decisions, perfectionism, fear of failure, black-and-white thinking, catastrophizing, and caretaking. Neurotic ambivalence is often the result of early learning, which, as established in the previous pages, can be resistant to change because of brain functioning. It can also be experienced by people who are highly sensitive and therefore harm avoidant, or simply because one doesn't have skills for dealing with ambivalence. An example of neurotic ambivalence is a parent who wants his child to become responsible and autonomous but is overly protective because of exaggerated fears about potential dangers.

The Borderline Condition

You may have noticed that the cognitions related to pathological ambivalence sound similar to splits that have traditionally been observed among people with borderline personality disorder (BPD). The borderline condition, as defined by Kernberg (1985) and later expanded by Marsha Linehan (1993), is said to occur when a child is raised in an environment that is not sufficiently validating, resulting in certain needs going unmet. In this conceptualization, identity becomes intertwined with conflicting needs, and the person develops a way of interacting with oneself and others that is highly resistant to change.

The focus in the past has been on the invalidating environment, and the folklore for decades was that people with this condition were very difficult to treat. Linehan was instrumental in changing this notion by developing specific and effective strategies to increase the chances that people with this diagnosis could in fact develop satisfying lives.

I also used to assume that the childhood of a person who developed borderline features had to be full of trauma; however, as I've learned more about brain functioning and worked with a wider variety of individuals, I've come to believe that it is possible to develop a personality disorder because of extreme sensitivity under normal levels of stress. Thus, I focus on the second part of the proposition related to what is "sufficiently" validating and believe that this varies greatly depending on the sensitivity of the child. One review of genetic epidemiological studies concluded that all 10 personality disorders classified in the 4th edition of the *Diagnostic and Statistical Manual of Mental Disorders* were modestly to moderately heritable (Reichnorn-Kiennerud, 2010). Kendler and Prescott (2006), in their book *Genes, Environment, and Psychopathology*, concluded that genetic factors can control an individual's sensitivity to the environment, that is, genetic factors influence or alter an organism's response to environmental stressors. Multiple lines of evidence have suggested that dysfunction in the serotonin system is associated with characteristics common in people with BPD and that genes linked to the function of this neurotransmitter can be considered candidate genes for developing the disorder (Ni et al., 2007). In 2009, Ni and his colleagues looked at serotonin genes and gene–gene interactions in a matched case–control study and concluded that serotonin genes may play a role in the susceptibility to BPD (Ni, Chan, Chan, McMain, & Kennedy, 2009). This line of research in important in the context of this book, in that it can provide counter-evidence to the scripts that may have been developed by the client with BPD, such as "I was treated poorly by my parents because I am inherently bad." It is helpful for people with this condition to see that they may have been more sensitive to the environment than the average person, thus making misattributions about their experiences. These misattributions can be reevaluated and the story rewritten.

Dissociation

Dissociation and DID occur when identity or self has become so splintered that some parts of the self can operate with needs and intentions completely separate from other parts of the self. This can occur with varying levels of co-consciousness. The phenomenon of dissociation was introduced by Pierre Janet at the end of the 19th century (LeBlanc, 2001). Dissociation may result when a person experiences something so intolerable that she is unable to process or integrate what happened. Dissociation also exists on a continuum from normal to extremely pathological, the latter possibly resulting in DID. Although this condition is important to assess, my interventions proceed in much the same way regardless of the diagnosis. I work to integrate ambivalence regardless of whether the parts have co-consciousness.

In summary, ambivalence takes many forms and exists on a continuum. The severity of the ambivalence will always be determined by an interplay of many factors related to environment and genetics. These factors are explored in more detail in the next chapter.

The Development of Pathological Ambivalence

My theory of the development of pathological ambivalence is as follows:

> *When a sensitive child is raised in an environment that is not sufficiently validating and empathic, certain needs go unmet, which may result in rigidity or separation among parts. The child will create a narrative (affected by age of experienced unmet needs) about how best to function in the world based on her sensitivity, early experiences, and unmet needs. Typically, the adult child then has two strong, but paradoxical, needs: to continue believing the old story while conversely hoping for the unmet needs to be met. These conflicting needs lead to ambivalence that may become pathological.*

Although simply put, there is much to understand about this definition. In the next chapter, I describe each component of this theory and review related theories that have influenced its development. You may notice that part of the theory is similar to Kernberg's (1975) and Linehan's (1993) concepts described earlier. However, clients can present with pathological ambivalence due to a variety of factors and with a variety of diagnoses.

Chapter 2: The Theory of Pathological Ambivalence

In the last chapter, I provided a fairly short description of how pathological ambivalence is developed. Now we will take each aspect of the theory and explore it in greater detail to understand the factors that are involved, as well as the theoretic background and research supporting this conceptualization.

The Sensitive Child

When a sensitive child is raised in an environment that is not sufficiently validating and empathic, certain needs go unmet.

In the definition of pathological ambivalence stated in the last chapter, it is important to note that there is an interplay between the invalidating environment and the level of sensitivity in the child. Everyone experiences environmental stress, some obviously much greater than others. However, individual factors greatly affect a person's resilience in coping with that stress. A sensitive child is more affected by the invalidation than is a less sensitive child. Although there aren't really good ways to quantify the relative proportions of environmental stress and one's sensitive nature in experiencing difficulties, I've come to believe that this is less important to therapeutic outcome than I once thought. It's sufficient to know that it's always in play.

The Highly Sensitive Person

Some people are born into the world with more sensitivity to stimuli than others. Highly sensitive people are more reactive and harm-avoidant than the average person. Some people jump at the slightest threat, while you'd have to light a fire under other people's chairs to get them to stand up. To illustrate this point, I like to talk about my two cats. If I drop a glass and it breaks, one of my cats, Domino, jumps about 5 feet into the air and runs out of the room. The other, Indy, swishes his tail and gives me a Garfield the Cat look that seems to say, "Did you really just knock over that glass?" I seriously believe he sometimes rolls his eyes at me. These two cats have lived in the same environment since they were just a few weeks old, but they are wired very differently. It's similar with people.

Early in my career, I was heavily influenced by Alice Miller's book, *Drama of the Gifted Child* (1981). She uses the term *gifted* to describe children who are more sensitive, intelligent, and aware than other children. These types of children become overly attuned to their parents' expectations to the detriment of their own identity development. Although Miller focused heavily on the stress or trauma in the environment as hurting these children, I was fascinated by the concept of highly sensitive people. She suggested that when these sensitive individuals are not parented according to their unique needs, they grow up to feel empty and unable to sense their own worth without constant approval from others.

Similarly, in 1996, Elaine Aron wrote *The Highly Sensitive Person*. Highly sensitive people, referred to as HSPs, are born with high sensory processing sensitivity. She describes HSPs as being sensitive to light, sound, and smells, and thus they may startle easily. She reports that about 20% of the population are HSPs who process sensory data more efficiently (it takes less stimulation to elicit processing) due to biological differences in their nervous systems. Subsequent brain imaging studies have added evidence to many of her concepts (Zeff, 2004) such as the serotonin effect described later in the chapter.

I believe that these people are also more insightful and more aware of nuances in the environment, such as other people's feelings, which is both a blessing and a burden. Because of their increased sensitivity, they are more vulnerable to stress in the environment (family problems, abuse, disasters, teasing, and bullying) and are naturally more likely to develop harm-avoidant coping mechanisms such as perfectionism (avoiding making mistakes), social withdrawal and shyness, hesitancy to verbalize emotions, and implementing caretaking behaviors to manage their sensitivity.

It is easy to see why this characteristic can be a burden and how these children can be traumatized by events that might not be as problematic for others. It also helps explain why many of these children struggle with perfectionism, as they take things to heart more quickly and deeply. Finally, one can see why these children might be susceptible to looking for ways of controlling themselves and their environment in an attempt to minimize the stress they experience.

This is in no way to suggest that they are *too* sensitive. People with this sensitivity are often told that they are too sensitive, they worry too much, make a mountain out of a molehill. I was actually called a "worry wart." What an awful phrase. These people are just as sensitive as they are born to be, and this biological sensitivity cannot be changed. There are wonderful advantages to being highly sensitive, and I would bet that most people who go into helping fields such as psychology or nursing, for example, are highly sensitive. Where would the world be without us? But we are challenged to learn effective ways to cope with our sensitivity, so that we don't break under the pressure—or, as I like to put it, spring a leak!

The Role of Serotonin

As mentioned in Chapter 1, research has found a connection between serotonin and the development of many psychiatric disorders such as eating disorders (Steiger, 2004), obsessive-compulsive disorder, mood disorders, posttraumatic stress disorder, and others (Mushtaq & Mushtaq, 2011). In general, producing sufficient levels of serotonin is related to feeling calm, achieving a sense of contentment, quality of sleep, and sensitivity to the environment. Additionally, the study of gene-by-environment interactions has gained momentum in the field of serotonin research. Caspi and his colleagues (2010) reviewed research about one of the most extensive areas of inquiry: variation in the promoter region of the serotonin transporter gene (*SLC6A4*; also known as *5-HTT*) and its contribution to stress sensitivity. Individuals having the serotonin low expressing short gene, referred to as the short allele (or S allele), were found to have an increased sensitivity to stress.

These studies, and many others, are showing that there are genetic factors related to how sensitive our patients may be to the environment in which they live, which is both a blessing and a burden. Evidence of marked variability in response among different people exposed to the same environmental risk implies that individual differences in genetic susceptibility might be at work. Acevedo and her colleagues (2014) used functional magnetic resonance imaging (fMRI) to study sensory processing sensitivity and concluded that the polymorphism of 5-HTT involved having stronger emotional reactions, processing of sensory information more deeply, being more aware of environmental subtleties, and being easily overstimulated. A related and fascinating study found that depending on the environmental stimuli, there were positive and negative benefits to having this gene (Fox, Zouqkou, Ridgewell, & Garner, 2011). Changes in attentional bias were greater in people with the low-expression form of the serotonin transporter gene in that they were faster to learn fear and develop neural circuits that are more sensitive to threat; however, the S allele carriers were also more responsive to positive training. The researchers concluded that these individuals were more tuned into their surroundings whether negative or positive.

The Invalidating Environment

When a sensitive child is raised in an environment that is not sufficiently validating and empathic, certain needs go unmet.

Much has been written and studied about the effects of maltreatment on children. Exposure to traumatic events activate the body's biological stress response systems and adversely affect childhood brain development (De Bellis, 2001). In an analysis of peer-reviewed studies on these adverse effects, De Bellis and Zisk, (2014) found studies demonstrating that maltreatment could lead to chronically elevated levels of corticotropin releasing hormone (CHR) causing generalized arousal, anxiety, aggression, and hypervigilance as well as decreased oxytocin production, memory problems, lower IQ, and lowered immunity.

Another pertinent area of research to our topic is in the area of trauma on the production of serotonin. As noted earlier, some people are born with differences in the HTPP gene related to serotonin production, but trauma also can dysregulate serotonin in humans. Children who are carriers of the S allele had a higher risk of developing depressive and suicidal symptoms when exposed to stressful life events. This gene × environment effect was related to trauma, age of trauma, duration of trauma and trauma type (Karg, Burmeister, Shedden, & Sen, 2011).

The Multiplicity of Human Personality

Certain needs go unmet, which can result in rigidity or separation among parts.

The second major factor related to the development of pathological ambivalence is the fact that all people have parts. When a child experiences unmet needs due to sensitivity and/or trauma, resulting confusion about these needs often ensues, manifesting as rigidity in the child's ego state development. The following theories have contributed to our understanding of this phenomena and the development of my theory of pathological ambivalence.

Early Psychoanalytic Theory

The first theorist to postulate the concept of personality comprising multiple parts was Sigmund Freud. To Freud, the patient's resistance occurred as the result of an intrapsychic impasse, reached between two or more conflicting agencies. Freud (1959a) wrote that "psychoanalysis … maintains that the isolation and unconsciousness of one group of ideas have been caused by an active opposition on the part of other groups" (p. 109). (This sounds remarkably like ambivalence to me!) Freud named one psychic agency the *repressing consciousness*, and the other agency the *unconscious*, which he eventually referred to as the *id* (1959b). The two competing parties strive for a compromise that will maximize drive satisfaction while minimizing resultant pain. Freud theorized that psychopathology was due to unsuccessful compromises.

Freud developed the concept of *working through*, which allowed patients to recognize and understand their resistance (Freud, 1959c).

> Conceived as the labor of the patient, rather than as an analytic technique, working through consists of two phases: recognizing resistances (insight) and overcoming resistances (change). … Finally, the concept of working through gives evidence for the idea of a will to recover which, in the psychoanalytic situation, becomes a will to remember. (Sedler, 1983, p. 73)

With his theory of the id, ego, and superego, Freud developed one of the first and definitely most famous conceptualizations of personality as being composed of different parts with potentially conflicting needs. He paved the way for many theorists and psychotherapists to begin understanding the complexities of human personality, including harm avoidance and the need to reduce anxiety, sometimes even through irrational means. It also informs the role of compromise among parts as one of the most efficient ways of managing ambivalence and as the ultimate goal. Psychoanalysis, therefore, involved facilitating adaptive compromises.

A more recent conceptualization (Wachtel, 1982) is that resistance occurs because of a developmental arrest in the functioning of the ego, specifically a failure in separation/individuation (2–3 years old) and is defined as all those conscious or unconscious emotions, attitudes, ideas, thoughts, or actions that operate against progress. Resistance is a defense (the need to protect self) that is expressed in the context of transference (the relationship with the therapist. Personally, I think negative transference is most likely to occur when the patient is highly ambivalent. I talk more about common mistakes that therapists make when encountering ambivalence in Chapter 4.

Over time the psychoanalytic viewpoint has shifted away from regarding resistance as a recalcitrant, oppositional tendency on the part of the patient, to acknowledging its inevitability and ubiquity. Resistance should be greeted as a therapist's friend, not as an enemy. It is the way in which clients present themselves to the world in general, and to the therapist in particular (Messer, 2002).

Transactional Analysis

In transactional analysis (TA), Eric Berne (1961) conceptualized the ego states as parent, child, and adult rather than id, ego, and superego. He defined an *ego state* as a consistent pattern of feeling and experience directly related to a corresponding consistent pattern of behavior. The parent ego state represents a massive collection of recordings in the brain (e.g., "Never talk to strangers") of *external* events (generally actions of parental figures, hence the label *parent ego state*) experienced or perceived in approximately the first 5 years of life. As these events are recorded without question and without analysis, one can consider that they are imposed on the child. The child ego state, also developing from birth to age 5, represents the recordings in the brain of the *internal* events associated with the corresponding external events the child experiences, such as "When Dad gets mad, I feel really scared." Stated another way, stored in the child ego state are the *emotions* or *feelings* that accompanied external events.

The beginning of the *adult ego state* occurs around age 1 year when the child learns that she can control certain aspects of the environment. Adult ego state data grow out of the child's ability to see what is different from what he or she was taught (parent ego state) or felt (child ego state). Harris (1967), in his classic book *I'm Okay, You're Okay*, describes the adult ego state as "a data-processing computer, which grinds out decisions after computing the information from three sources: the parent, the child, and the data which the adult has gathered and is gathering" (1967, p. 32).

In TA, resistance occurs when parent, child, and adult ego states are not cooperating. It is easy to see that ambivalence can occur if a child is introjecting his parents' rules at the same time that the child is in conflict with the rule, such as "I can't have dessert before dinner, and I want the cake now."

Although Freud's and Berne's ego states are highly analogous, I find that Berne's conceptualization of parent, adult, and child has more face validity than Freud's nomenclature of id, ego, and superego. However, it is still somewhat confusing, because the parent ego state and child ego state are both said to have formed between the ages of 1 and 5 (i.e., when the person is a child). Similarly, the adult ego state begins to form at about 1 year old. It's confusing to me to consider the adult ego state as forming at such an early age, considering what we know about brain development. I prefer referring to ego states based on cognitive and brain development and using the terms *child*, *adolescent*, and *adult* to describe differing ego states that are primarily formed at the actual corresponding ages.

Ego States as Related to Brain Development

In my conceptualization, the child ego state forms first while the brain is primarily using limbic system and brain stem functions. In this state, the person is unable to think abstractly and thus is very egocentric in her cognitions. Egocentricity, at the earliest age, is characterized by the inability to untangle subjective schemas from objective reality and an inability to understand or assume any perspective other than one's own. The child relies mostly on instinct and reaction and is subject to strong and rapidly shifting emotional experiences without the benefit of the ability to consider reasons for the experiences. Thus, children at this age are extremely vulnerable to environment.

Later in this phase, awareness about causality begins to form, but there is only awareness causality as it relates to the self. The child believes that his unique experiences are representative of all people's experiences. I remember having a principal in the first grade whose name started with a "B." He left during this year and was replaced by a second principal whose name also started with a "B." When talking with one of my friends from a different school, I asked her what her principal's name was, and she said Mr. Davis. I remember telling her that she was wrong because principal's names had to start with a "B." I was so certain of this that I almost convinced her!

For individuals with pathological ambivalence, the child ego state is likely characterized by fear and shame. Early imprinting of safety or danger occurs during this phase and may or may not be connected to memory. Shame may be a strong component of this ego state as children are assuming responsibility for negative things that have happened. On the other hand, the child ego state also contains a strong ability and wish to connect to others even at their own expense. Survival for babies and young children is dependent on connection to an adult; thus, we are hardwired to connect at almost any cost.

During the formation of the adolescent ego state, egocentrism gradually decreases. As he heads into adolescence, beginning around age 10 or 11, a person begins developing the ability to think abstractly and can begin forming rules in his mind about how to best operate in his environment. There is still a measure of egocentricity ("it will never happen to me"), but the child is beginning to use the posterior cerebral cortex. This part of the brain utilizes the five senses to create our perception of the world. It is referred to as the new mammalian brain because it is present in primates, although it is more developed in human beings. At this age, he begins to notice patterns and to think about the best way to interact with his world. Thinking tends to be black-and-white absolutes, creating rules based on earlier experiences. Cognitions are likely to be highly characterized by rules that include words like *should*, *always*, and *never*. For very sensitive individuals, even positive messages from others can turn into rigid rules such as "you can do anything you want in life" can be interpreted as "I must do something remarkable."

As an adolescent, a person may begin saying statements to himself such as, "To make Dad happy, I must excel in sports." Or "People will think I'm silly, so I should be quiet." Additionally, the quality of the thoughts related to these rules and beliefs are often patterned after perceptions of early caregivers. For instance, if mom called the client names, then the client is likely to use the same names and even tone of voice when criticizing herself. It should be noted, however, that often the adolescent voice is even more rigid or critical than that of the caregivers in that she had to learn to beat them to the punch: "I'll hit me before you hit me." For example, an adolescent may develop perfectionism in an attempt to avoid ever hearing criticism. The parent may never have intended for the child to feel that she had to be perfect but did things that the adolescent learned to avoid by attempting to be perfect. Another example is if a parent occasionally made the mistake of saying something like, "Why did you *do* something so stupid?" which then translated into the adolescent as "I *am* stupid." Therefore, it is the adolescent part of us that has developed a narrative to live by or, as Adler referred to it, a "story of my life."

We are operating from the adult ego state when we are using our prefrontal lobes, which are the last to come *on line*, so to speak, as our brain is developing. I refer to this ego state with varying terms that I've gathered from other readings such as *wise mind*, *observing self*, and *nurturing parent*. In late adolescence and early adulthood we develop the capabilities often grouped together by the term executive functioning. This is an umbrella term for the management (regulation, control) of cognitive processes, including working memory, choosing a focus of attention, switching focus, observing oneself, time management, and problem-solving, as well as planning and execution. Whew, that's a lot! The prefrontal lobes are the part of the brain that we are using when we are observing our own mind and choosing on what to place our attention.

As described earlier, some people have more difficulty using the prefrontal lobes due to age, attention-deficit/hyperactivity disorder, level of serotonin, or connectivity. These individuals may have less neuronal connectivity between the limbic system and prefrontal lobes, making it more difficult to manage emotions and choose a new course of action. The good news is that the brain is constantly forming new pathways, and through mindfulness practices, this connectivity can be increased. The 3-minute mindfulness practice described previously can help with building this connectivity.

Table 2.1 summarizes some of the general distinctions of each ego state. Even though the adolescent ego state is characterized by rules, this doesn't mean that the person never feels emotion when in the adolescent state. Most of the rules are triggered by emotion.

Table 2.1. The Ego States			
	Child ego state	Adolescent ego state	Adult ego state
Analogous Concepts	Emotional mind	Reasonable mind	Wise mind
	Inner child	Narratives, scripts, rules	Observing self
	Child ego state (Berne)		Mindsight
		Parent ego state (Berne)	Nurturing parent
		Critical Parent	
Characteristics	Needs	Rules	Wisdom
	Wishes	Perceived expectations	Calm and contentment
	Desires		
	Emotion	Rigidity	Flexibility
	Instinct	Cognition and anxiety	Emotion and cognition
	Shame and sadness	Learning	Experience and values
	dependence	Anger	Acceptance
		Independence	Interdependence

Gestalt Theory

Gestalt theory has in its name a description of the purpose of therapy. A *gestalt* is defined as an organized whole that is perceived as more than the sum of its parts. Resistance is depicted as parts that have not been integrated into a whole. In gestalt therapy, the only goal is *awareness,* assuming that full awareness brings about change when needed, by leading to integration of parts or resolving ambivalence. *Resistance* is considered to be one part of a polarity consisting of an impulse and resistance to the impulse. Seen as a dichotomy, resistance is often treated as "bad" by the clinician and, in such a context, often turns out to be nothing more than patients following their own wishes rather than being open to the therapist's suggestions. Conversely, considering resistance as part of a polarity, the resistance can be viewed as having as much importance to the treatment as the healthy behaviors.

Early gestalt theorists (Perls, Hefferline, & Goodman, 1951) conceptualized resistance as an unaware conflict within an individual, a permanent avoidance that limits the individual's contact with self. This process commonly is referred to as *resistance to awareness.*

Other gestalt authors (Latner, 2000; Polster & Polster, 1973) believed *resistance* to be the client's struggle to balance stability versus change. Resistance is the person's self-protective attempt to avoid the anxiety that life change involves. Because gestalt theory states that all parts need to work together to make a functioning, whole, system, gestalt psychologists have developed extremely helpful strategies for integrating ambivalence. These strategies include Empty Chair, Body Techniques, Here and Now (mindfulness techniques), and Exaggeration. Many strategies described in Part II are consistent with these techniques.

Object Relations Theory

Object relations theory provides a bridge between the concept of personality comprising parts and the influence of early experiences on the nature of those parts. Object relations theory focuses on the child's relationship with his caregivers during critical developmental years. The theory suggests that the way people relate to others and to situations in their adult lives is shaped by family experiences during infancy and early childhood. Images of people and events experienced at this stage turn into *objects* (or parts) in the unconscious that the person carries into adulthood. These objects are later used by the subconscious to predict people's behavior in their social relationships and interactions (St. Clair, 2000). For example, an adult who experienced neglect or abuse in infancy and early childhood would expect similar behavior from others.

In the context of object relations theory, resistance occurs in psychotherapy when the patient is assuming (consciously or unconsciously) that the interaction in the therapeutic relationship will have similar qualities to their early relationships. There is a defensive (protective) need to see the relationship in light of early relationships, and anxiety is experienced when trying to give it up. Therapy would require a working through of the internal object to form new representations for relationships (Summers, 1999).

The Development of Narrative

The child will create a narrative about how best to function in the world based on her sensitivity, early experiences, and unmet needs.

Influenced by the vulnerability factors described earlier, a child develops schemas about how to be in the world. Schemas comprise beliefs, narratives, scripts, and emotions that may be learned at a very early age and then reinforced through repetition. These schemas become so *hardwired* that the person may not even be consciously aware that they are operating. They may have several significant neural pathways, or what I like to refer to as "brain real estate" devoted to these schemas.

The narrative is the part of the schema which contains the story that has been guiding the person since childhood. These narratives incorporate beliefs about self, beliefs about others, beliefs about emotions, and beliefs about the world that will greatly impact the way the person functions in life. This narrative may manifest itself in both *intra*personal functioning and *inter*personal functioning, generally involving a shame-based identity, the communication of mixed messages, projecting assumptions onto others, and splitting. If the trauma was excessively painful, part or parts of the narrative may be dissociated.

Adlerian Theory

Alfred Adler (1964) initially collaborated with Freud in the development of his thoughts about personality. Although he agreed with Freud that personality is highly affected by childhood events, he eventually shifted his focus from how the personality is made of parts to how schemas develop, particularly those related to feelings of social inferiority. Adler theorized that a person naturally develops a "story of my life." This story is then repeated inwardly to warn him or to comfort him, to keep him concentrated on his goal, to prepare him, by means of past experiences, and to meet the future with an already tested style of action. Adler developed the concept of private intelligence, which was later termed "private logic," to describe the fictional line of reasoning that proceeds from a person's private valuation of self, others, and the world and what life requires of him (Griffith & Powers, 2007, p. 81). Adler believed that problems develop when people create symptoms as a means of protecting their fragile self-esteem based on this private logic, which consists of the hidden reasons that justify a person's actions, deeds, and thoughts, or the belief that what worked as a child should work as an adult. These safeguarding tendencies can maintain a dysfunctional style of life while functioning as an attempt to protect oneself (Griffith & Powers, 2007).

Like others, Adler viewed the first 5 years of life as central in the development of personality. During these years, the experiences that a child has will create a filter or lens, if you will, based on the child's early conceptualization of both self and the world. If one is fortunate, the lenses may be rose-colored, although often they are not. Adler called this the *schema of perceptions*, or the idea that individual perception is limited by the discrepancy between reality and the person's perception of reality. For mentally healthy people, this discrepancy is relatively small; for psychologically disturbed people, the discrepancy is much greater (Marcus & Rosenberg, 1998).

Dreikurs (1967) wrote that resistance occurs when there is a discrepancy between the goals of the therapist and the patient's goal of maintaining his sense of self or story. Accordingly, resistance occurs when the client's "private logic" is no longer adaptive but is still in operation.

Narrative Theory

Similar to Adlerian theory, narrative theory is based on the premise that as humans, we seek to make meaning of our experiences by linking events together to form a story (Morgan, 2000). Narrative theory holds that our identities are shaped by the accounts of our lives found in our stories. Although narratives appear definitive, they actually are pliable and fluid and therefore can be rewritten. In narrative therapy, the problem is separated from the person through objectification or externalization, giving the person more power to change behavior (White & Epston, 1990). A benefit of narrative therapy is that by telling their stories, clients may increase awareness of, or even uncover, things of which they were previously unaware. In this approach, resistance is seen as the client's assumption that the story is synonymous with self, and therefore very difficult to change.

Narrative therapy researchers Ribeiro, Goncalves, Bras, and Sousa (2016) conducted a study in which they monitored return-to-problem behaviors in 10 clients treated by the same therapist. In the cases that did not improve, the researchers observed that therapist interventions were more likely to meet the client's problems by *challenging* maneuvers, followed by the client invalidating the therapeutic intervention. They described a process through which a person may break temporarily from her problematic self-narrative as a result of therapy, but this may generate feelings of uncertainty and instability that needed to be recognized. There was a pull to return to the status quo. Ribeiro and his colleagues wrote that "the persistent expression of two opposing aspects of the self, which pulls the clients towards two distinct directions, may be conceptualized as a way of resisting change" (p. 174).

Cognitive Viewpoint

Because narrative comprises cognitions or scripts, it is helpful to look at cognitive viewpoints in understanding resistance and the development of pathological ambivalence. Lazarus and Fay (1982) wrote that "the concept of 'resistance' is probably the most elaborate rationalization that therapists employ to explain their treatment failures" (p. 115). He believed that it was a convenient excuse for the therapist's lack of understanding or skill. Obviously, the responsibility, as he saw it, was on the therapist who had failed to give adequate rationale for the assigned homework. Lazarus may have been one of the first theorists to suggest that we shouldn't consider resistance something that the client was doing to us, such as resisting our interventions.

Another cognitive viewpoint is that resistance is caused by maladaptive, distorted, conceptualizations and dysfunctional beliefs. In his book *Overcoming Resistance in Cognitive Therapy*, Leahy (2003) described seven dimensions of resistance from the cognitive perspective. Some of these include habitual ways of viewing self through personal schemas developed early in life, an inability to handle emotional intensity (maybe a highly sensitive individual), and the need for self-consistency (which I view as heavily tied to brain functioning).

Sims and Lorenzi (1992) similarly defined resistance as dysfunctional cognitive schemas developed early in life that are resistant to change because of the protective nature of the schemas. New information that falls within an individual's schema is easily remembered and incorporated into his worldview. However, when new information does not fit a schema, resistance may occur. The most common reaction is simply to ignore or quickly forget the new information. This can happen on a deep level, such that an individual does not even perceive the new information.

Early maladaptive schemas can be conceptualized as broad and pervasive themes or patterns made up of memories, feelings, sensations, and thoughts regarding oneself and one's relationships with others (Young, Klosko, & Weishaar, 2003). They presumably develop during childhood or adolescence, are elaborated on throughout life, and are dysfunctional in that they lead to self-defeating behavior. Examples include schemata of abandonment/instability, mistrust/abuse, emotional deprivation, and defectiveness/shame.

John's story illustrates how early experiences can affect the narrative a child develops, which can then lead to extreme ambivalence in adulthood.

> *When I was 3 years old, my parents decided that they no longer wanted to be together. It was confusing and upsetting for me. I wasn't old enough to realize that it was their shortcoming rather than my own, and I began to believe that I must not be lovable. I adjusted to this belief by assuming that the only way that I could be safe was to keep my distance from people and be on guard for messages related to the probability that I was not*

lovable. I also overcompensated by constantly trying to earn love from these people, even though I didn't trust them.

I was extremely ambivalent about relationships. I unknowingly created a story that went something like, "Dad left and Mom withdrew from me because I'm not loveable enough. I need to work real hard to make people like me so that other people I meet will not leave. I won't be loved for who I am, but if I work hard enough, they might at least want to be around me. However, I should be cautious and not completely vulnerable because other people can't be trusted fully and will probably leave eventually. I should not burden others with my own thoughts and feelings or they might leave sooner."

I was hesitant to allow people to get too close since I "knew" that others would probably reject me. When they did, I believed that it reinforced the truth of my childhood. This belief became so much a part of me that it was like a chronic feeling, operating even when I was unaware that it was in my thoughts. Every time I met someone, I was somewhat reserved, regardless of the way that they were interacting with me. I didn't realize at the time that these beliefs I had formed years ago made me interact in such a way that resulted in making trustworthy people to want to eventually leave me. I believed that they were leaving because I was inherently unlovable, not because of the way I was acting in the present moment. Thus, no matter how hard I tried, they would still leave. It was a downward spiral that left me trying harder and harder to be attentive without expecting anything in return; then being rejected anyway. Then as they left, of course, my belief was once again reinforced. Deep down I believed that I would be alone forever.

The schemas (thoughts, beliefs, emotions, and body sensations) that John developed had become so much a part of the way he approached life that it was, in large part, subconscious. Changing these schemas will involve becoming aware of how and why they developed, and reevaluating the validity of his beliefs. Although these schemas are deeply embedded, research has shown that the brain is always changing, a concept referred to as *plasticity*.

Neuroplasticity

Neuroplasticity or brain plasticity refers to the brain's ability to change its structure due to both genetic and environmental factors. What actually changes is the strength of the connections between neurons and synapses that are engaged together. The more you repeat something, the more connections are made. In the first neuroimaging investigation of the effects of cognitive behavior therapy (CBT), magnetic resonance imaging was used to show that CBT could change the neural correlates of spider phobia in 12 patients. They concluded that CBT had the potential to modify the dysfunctional neural circuitry associated with anxiety disorders (Paquette et al., 2003). It has been postulated that the mechanism behind the effectiveness of cognitive therapy could be an increase in prefrontal function (DeRubeis, Siegle, & Hollon, 2008) or focused awareness on new thoughts. Hanson (2011) reviewed 20 studies conducted between 1992 and 2010 on brain changes after psychotherapy for depression, anxiety disorders, and borderline personality disorder and concluded that CBT, dialectical behavior therapy, psychodynamic psychotherapy, and interpersonal psychology could all alter brain functioning in these patients.

When we learn something new, there must be changes in the neural circuitry to correspond to the new learning, thus shaping our brain. Our understanding of plasticity has changed through the years as first being understood as a developmental function. Later studies revealed that the brain can change after a brain injury and in more recent years, researchers have found that changes occur later in life (Mateer & Kerns, 2000). Researchers are utilizing the concept of neuroplasticity to target certain goals such as in the area of speech pathology (McDonald & Carroll, 1992). Finally, every moment of learning provides an opportunity for the brain to shift from potentially interfering thoughts. That is, each time the brain strengthens a connection to advance mastery of a skill, it also weakens other connections of neurons that weren't used at that moment (Merzinich, 2013).

Taken together, these studies offer a basis for strategies which enable clients to purposefully change the structure of their brain toward desired goals. Strategies will be discussed in Chapter 7 for facilitating the rewriting of the narratives and thus shifting the entire schema.

Narrative Affected by Age

The nature of the narrative can be strongly affected by the individual's age at the time the needs first go unmet.

Developmental factors related to age can influence later difficulties with ambivalence to change. Early childhood is marked by egocentrism because of limits in brain capacity. Anderman and Anderman (2009) described egocentrism as the inability to differentiate between self and other. More specifically, it is the inability to untangle subjective schemas from objective reality, coupled with an inability to understand or assume any perspective other than their own. This is why when bad things happen, depending on the cognitive development of the child, he may believe that it's his fault and that he's not good enough or is unlovable. As he heads into adolescence, he develops the capacity to think abstractly and can begin forming rules in his mind about how to best operate in his environment. These rules are based on the earlier beliefs. As an adolescent, he may begin saying to himself statements such as, "To make Dad happy, I must be perfect" or "People will think I'm silly, so I should be quiet."

If the stories we tell ourselves go back to childhood, they are based on the limited cognitive functioning during the developmental stage in which the learning occurred. These stories can be inaccurate and thus affect us quite negatively. Additionally, relative to the number of times they've been repeated in our thoughts, they have produced strong neural pathways. I explain this to patients when they say they can't believe positive affirmations about themselves. I say, "Of course you can't yet, but you wouldn't want an adolescent telling you what to believe, would you? Maybe it's time to tell that adolescent part of you a new story."

Piaget (1954, 1964) developed a theory of cognitive development, which he then dramatically demonstrated through a series of experiments. By closely watching children play, he was able to observe cognitive shifts as the child matured. He described cognitive development as a series of stages.

A brief review of these stages illustrates how environment and brain development can interact to greatly influence how we perceive ourselves and the world. For instance, if a child is experiencing stressful situations during the *sensorimotor stage* of development (birth to 2 years), which is characterized by extreme egocentrism, she has no ability to understand the experience or credit it to anyone other than herself. The stress is then recorded in the neural pathways and experienced as a general sense of endangerment.

I have worked with several girls who were adopted from foreign countries. One of these girls has scars on her wrists and ankles that her adoptive mother reports were there when she was adopted at 8 months. They assume she was tied down as an infant. Whatever experiences she had before 8 months are imprinted neurologically, and they continue to affect her, even though she has no cognitive awareness of the early experience. She suffers with a pervasive and consuming experience of danger, which has expressed itself as a severe anxiety disorder for which no other cause can be found.

Reasoning at the sensorimotor stage is very limited. There is no ability to understand cause and effect, although the brain is rapidly developing associations. Therefore, if dad yelled when the child was picking up a toy, then the child is likely to assume that picking up the toy caused dad to yell—even if he had been yelling at someone else or at the TV.

In the *preoperational stage*, from approximately ages 2 to 4 years, the child assumes that other people see, hear, and feel exactly the same as he does. If something bad happens, he is likely to believe that he caused it, and therefore he is bad. Toxic shame has its origins in this phase, where a child may believe that if someone else does something wrong, it is his fault. Children's cognitions related to others' wrongdoing may focus on searching for explanations of how they caused the bad thing to happen. Additionally, a very sensitive child may internalize shame at this stage when a parent is simply trying to correct or teach. A schema of shame may develop separate from actual memories or cognitions. She might over-respond to the negative messages given at this age and less to the positive messages. I've worked with people who describe a pervasive sense of shame, even though they believe they were well-parented and have no history of abuse. This adds to their sense of shame because they feel they have no right to feel this way.

The *concrete operational stage* (preadolescence) is characterized by the application of logic in thinking, but this logic is still rudimentary. In this stage, the child assumes that if something often happens, then it will *always* happen. For example, if dad left and then grandfather died, all men will leave me. Under stress, children are likely to develop hardwired beliefs and rules about themselves and the world that are projected onto current situations.

The *formal operational stage* begins usually around the ages of 11 to 12 years and continues developing through adulthood. It is characterized by the child's ability to think creatively, use abstract reasoning, and imagine the outcome of particular actions (Piaget, 1972). Formal operations are what we apply when we pause and use mindfulness skills to analyze and respond to a situation in the moment, rather than from hardwired beliefs.

In summary, children are very vulnerable to developing narratives that lead to adult expressions of ambivalence based on the age at which they experienced stress and the level of cognitive development at that time. The associations formed during early cognitive development may not be readily apparent or seem logical to the adult who can process information much differently. The therapist can educate the client about this as a strategy for understanding how to resolve ambivalence.

Conflict Between Core Needs

Typically, the adult child then has two strong, but paradoxical, needs: to continue believing the old story, while conversely hoping for the unmet needs to be met. These conflicting needs lead to ambivalence that may become pathological.

Thus, ambivalence will clearly arise when, on one hand, there is a drive to maintain the status quo so that the pain of addressing the unmet need can be avoided, while on the other hand, there is a wish to have early needs met. Narratives that embody dysfunctional beliefs are responsible for the development of pathological ambivalence when they are in direct conflict with normal human needs. For example, a belief that no one can be trusted may be juxtaposed with the human need to feel connection to others. The alternating expressions of these needs are confusing to both patient and therapist, when the patient is expressing only one of the needs at a time, or alternating between the two without awareness of both. The expression of conflicting needs and beliefs are often misinterpreted as resistance to therapy.

Thus, change will involve significant conscious effort in building new neural pathways to support new beliefs and healthier functioning. It is important to do a thorough assessment of a person's beliefs early in the therapeutic process (see Chapter 5) to avoid interpreting the ambivalence as resistance and enable the client to increase awareness of conflicting needs. In summary, the person develops a narrative that leads to pathological ambivalence in the following form: *No one will care for my needs, but I secretly, maybe even unconsciously, crave the experience of being taken care of.*

Systemic Factors

Family Theory

Family theorists offer many different viewpoints on resistance but share the view of resistance as parts (members) of the family that aren't functioning well as a whole (Anderson & Stewart, 1983). When a family therapist doesn't understand the dynamics of the resistance, then change is less likely to occur. These viewpoints have also informed my theory of how ambivalence develops either between persons or within a person. The following are several definitions of resistance from various family therapy viewpoints:

1. Resistance occurs because of the drive for homeostasis. This relates to the idea that all change is met with ambivalence. For example, parents may reenact what they learned growing up. Or a very sensitive child may take on the role of feeling emotion for the entire family (Solomon, 1974).

2. Resistance occurs as a result of dysfunctional or rigid communication patterns. A parent may have a pattern of communicating to the other parent through the child. This concept came from strategic family therapy models first developed by Bateson and Hayley as part of the Palo Alto Group in the 1950s (Madanes, 1981; Nichols & Schwartz, 1912).

3. Resistance occurs because of problems in the structure of the hierarchy, or boundary problems between members (triangulation). One parent may desire a relationship focused more on friendship than parenting (Minuchin, 1974).
4. Resistance is attributed to secondary gains achieved by the targeted behavior, such as when secondary gratification outweighs desire to get better (Watzlavick, Weakland, & Fisch, 1974).
5. Resistance can be attributed to the phenomenon of induction, which Minuchin and Fishman (2004) defined as an impasse created by the therapist's becoming part of the family dysfunction. An example would be the therapist siding with one of the members, which can maintain dysfunctional family homeostasis.

Family therapists are uniquely situated to see resistance between parts in action and thus have developed many strategies aimed at integrating the parts of the family system. In this case, the parts are actual people who need to work together as a whole. One can imagine the complexities of working with families when you recognize that each person is a part of the whole and that each person comprises parts within oneself. Sometimes working with a child and adult part of each member of a couple is like having four people in the room rather than two! Having been trained as a family therapist, I began to apply some of the concepts from this field and converted some of the strategies to use with individuals struggling with discordant parts within themselves, such as learning to validate each part before problem-solving.

Homeostasis

As mentioned earlier, homeostasis is a central theme among family theorists' explanation for why families have difficulty with change. Homeostasis is a basic phenomenon in nature that applies to humans at every level of functioning from cellular to abstract thought. In pathological ambivalence, the drive for homeostasis manifests itself even in the face of dysfunction. This drive is rooted in brain functioning and can be observed in both individual functioning and interpersonal experiences. Because of my family therapy background, I have a strong appreciation for how this drive operates as a factor related to the development of ambivalence. I have presented several workshops on how to conduct individual psychotherapy from a systems perspective in which I encourage therapists to always consider the systems in which our clients have and are currently living. By doing so, therapists are more likely to remember that they are only receiving one perspective in their session and are less likely to make common mistakes in doing so. You'll read more about this in Chapters 5 and 6. If we aren't aware of the many ways the systems in which they live impacts our clients, our work with them can be ineffective and at times even harmful.

In summary, conceptualizing resistance as ambivalence (internal splitting, so to speak) will change the way you work with clients and reduce your frustration when confronting resistance. Integration of differing needs is the cornerstone for successful therapy with patients expressing pathological ambivalence.

Chapter **3: Common Forms of Ambivalence in Psychotherapy**

Ambivalence, regardless of the level of personality organization as described in Chapter 2, is experienced in psychotherapy in many forms. It is important to recognize these expressions as early as possible in the therapeutic experience.

Lack of Basic Knowledge or Skills

At times individuals are ambivalent about change simply because they perceive themselves as lacking the skills to bring about the change. This is the easiest form of ambivalence to resolve. Once it is determined that the difficulty is a lack of skills, providing skills should resolve the ambivalence. Some individuals, however, are hesitant to admit that they can't do something, especially if they believe that most people can, or that they should already know how. Unless this is assessed early in the process, the therapist is likely to attribute the lack of progress to resistance.

Carrie sought therapy for career counseling. She took the Strong-Campbell Interest Inventory, which confirmed her desire to go into sales. She made a plan with her therapist to write a résumé and to begin looking at job opportunities. Several weeks went by, during which she had "resisted" doing her homework. Conversation in therapy sessions centered on what had happened during the week that distracted her from writing her résumé. Finally, Carrie exclaimed that she was procrastinating because she had never written a résumé before and didn't know how to get started. The therapist had made the assumption that this well-spoken, apparently bright client had the basic knowledge to do this. Therefore, when giving homework assignments, it is important to simply ask whether the client knows how to get started on the homework or can predict any reason that it might not get done.

The Power Struggle

One of the most common mistakes therapists make in dealing with ambivalence in psychotherapy is to engage in a power struggle with a patient. Often when a patient is ambivalent, he may voice only one side of his ambivalence at a time. For example, if the patient says, "I am never going to get better," a caring therapist naturally wants to instill hope. However, as the therapist voices hope, she is taking the positive side of the ambivalence. Once the positive side of the ambivalence has been voiced, the other side needs to be voiced for the patient to feel fully understood. Consequently, the patient is likely to repeat the negative voice and may even state it more strongly. The power struggle develops as the therapist tries harder to win the argument for hope, leaving the patient to struggle to maintain his lack of hope. Instilling hope is an important therapeutic strategy; however, the timing is vitally important. If an attempt at instilling hope is met with resistance or "yes–butted," then another strategy needs to be substituted quickly.

Tracy's story will help illustrate this point. Tracy was a young woman struggling with severe panic disorder, substance abuse, and an eating disorder. She had been in several treatment programs with multiple relapses. Part of her history involved being sexually abused by a former therapist about 5 years earlier. She had pressed charges and testified against this man in court. He was found guilty and was currently in prison.

Tracy often vacillated between expressing anger and feeling shame. These two emotions are diametrically opposed. Anger implies the right to be treated well and the need for protection, while shame implies the opposite. It's interesting to note that she was given a diagnosis of borderline personality disorder (BPD) from a previous course of treatment, which may have been inaccurate, even though her behavior was consistent with some aspects of BPD. Conceptualizing her as struggling with pathological ambivalence informed a more effective treatment plan.

She spent about half of her time in sessions expressing anger regarding people who had let her down and the other half in shame, as if she deserved being treated badly. She would swing between the emotions, sometimes so much so that she asked me if I thought she was crazy. I responded that I did not think she was crazy, but I thought she was extremely ambivalent. When she would express her anger and I would attempt to validate her anger, she would swing to feeling shame. But when she was feeling shame and I tried to dissuade her of the feeling, she would switch to anger. It felt to me like we could never stay in sync and that she would discount anything I said. I realize now that I was just swinging with her. A typical conversation might go something like this:

Tracy: I am so angry that someone who was supposed to take care of me would actually harm me.

Me: He did harm you and that was wrong.

Tracy: No, it was my fault—I was an adult, I should've known better.

Me: It is common for people to feel shame after situations like this, but you must see that it wasn't your fault.

Tracy: But why would I feel shame when I am so angry that he would do this? I thought he cared about me.

Me: You have a right to feel angry, because your trust was betrayed.

Tracy: No, you don't understand. I was an adult. I shouldn't have let things happen.

Me: I do understand that it is normal for people to feel shame and anger in these kinds of situations.

Tracy: How could you possibly understand my feelings? It didn't happen to you and you weren't there. [Now she really had me! She wins!]

There were moments when it appeared that I had "won" the power struggle, convincing her that there was reason to believe that she had worth. And she would say something like, "I guess you're right, but I can't feel it, so something must be wrong with me." This was not a very satisfying win and it definitely didn't change anything.

In these conversations, I felt powerless, ineffective, and at times frustrated with her. Why wouldn't she let me help her?! Was she ever going to heal from this thing that, although horrible, happened so long ago? Was there something about me that kept her from trusting me? One time when I tried an object relations approach, I asked her that question. She actually told me it had no *f'ing* thing to do with me! That was one of those moments in life when you just wish the ground would open up and swallow you. But now, I look back at that moment and smile with fondness. She taught me so much!

Not only did these kinds of conversations happen between Tracy and me, they also happened in her group therapy. Other group members tried very hard to convince her that she should let go of the shame connected to the abuse by the therapist, that she had done nothing wrong, and that she had a right to feel angry. When they would get angry in her defense, she reacted by withdrawing. When others voiced her anger, she couldn't feel it because her mind responded to validation by feeling shame. When she did respond, she "yes-butted them" at every turn. She couldn't trust that they believed her, that they cared about her, or that they could possibly understand her situation.

Finally, after several sessions of feeling stuck with Tracy and realizing that she and I were both leaving sessions feeling frustrated with each other and with ourselves, I decided to totally go with her resistance. Frankly, this occurred more out of desperation than amazing wisdom on my part. So, when she started to express her shame about her relationship with the former therapist, I asked her, "Okay, what percentage of the situation do you think was your fault?" She stared at me and paused for a few minutes. My heart was beating faster than normal. I had no idea how she was going to respond. I was afraid that she would think I was "blaming the victim," something that I was loath to do.

When she finally spoke, it was with a soft voice, as opposed to the typically defensive or argumentative tone that she usually used. She said, "No one has ever asked me that. But if I think about it, I believe it's about 20% my fault." So we talked about the 20% that she perceived was her fault. This became an amazingly empowering session for her. It turns out that there was a small part of her that was very afraid that she might let herself get into that kind of situation again. Trying to talk her out of feeling that way was not helping at all. Being afraid to address this with her was neglecting a very hurt, scared, and childlike part of her.

I believe that Tracy's eating disorder was functioning as a communication from a part of herself, which believed that she had to be sick to protect herself from abuse and that she deserved punishment for the responsibility that she perceived was hers in the situation. Talking about the 20% that felt like her responsibility gave her hope that she would be better able to protect herself if a situation like this ever happened again. She needed to reassure herself that she had learned from the experience to better protect herself and to have clearer boundaries. Additionally, she began to explore things from her childhood that she thought had contributed to the 20% for which she felt responsible. She and I had been unable to delve into those issues because we had both been swinging to thoughts related to her being the victim and not to blame.

After that initial session of going with her resistance, she went into group therapy and told the group in a very matter-of-fact way that 20% of the situation had been her fault. She said it with such confidence that no one in the group disagreed. They, too, listened to her perspective fully. I realized that I had been engaged in a power struggle with Tracy based on my own value of never blaming the victim. This was not in her best interest, and one of us always lost. When I put this aside and joined her resistance, it became a turning point in her recovery.

As part of Tracy's process for termination, she wrote a letter to me summarizing our work together. She wrote,

> You helped me find strength within me that I never knew existed. You helped me to find my "voice" and to begin to listen to and trust my inner wisdom. You helped me to discover the balance ... to find the middle ground of nonjudgment. You never attempted to wrestle the disorder away from me [I guess she had forgotten those first few sessions] ... instead you helped me to find the will and desire to let go of the symptoms and to face what issues emerged over time.

I think I did these things by getting out of the way and helping her understand her ambivalence. I'm happy to say that she was still doing fine the last time I heard from her years later.

Manipulation

Another common manifestation of ambivalence in psychotherapy is manipulation—when someone attempts to get her needs met without asking directly. I educate my clients on the meaning of the word so that it doesn't have such a negative connotation. For instance, to manipulate is just to get something you need, such as manipulating a drawer to get a pen. Patients who are very ambivalent about their needs may feel that it isn't okay for them to ask directly; consequently, they believe they must resort to manipulation.

One example of a patient manipulating a therapist is someone who spends session after session talking about a crisis that happened that week. By focusing on the crises, the therapy seldom moves forward. Early in my career, I would be frustrated by this because I believed we could never get to the *real* therapy. I have since learned to use my frustration as a signal that the client may be feeling ambivalent about something, which we need to address. The therapist could ask the client what she thinks they would talk about if there had been no crisis this week, implying that talking about crises is actually controlling the session in some way. One patient told me, after several probing questions, that she didn't think I would be interested in her if she weren't in crisis. This was something that she had learned at an early age when her busy mother paid attention primarily when things were going wrong. This patient needed to know that she was uniquely interesting with or without a crisis but would never find that out with her current behavior. She believed she was doomed to forever having to be in crisis to experience herself as important. She was encouraged to talk about the feelings of not being important rather than try to *make* (a manipulation) herself important every week.

Splitting

Splitting occurs when a patient is unable to tolerate the experience of ambivalence and grasp clear boundaries. I introduce here early theories of object relations to help the reader understand how and why this behavior might develop. Mahler, Pine, and Bergman (1975) wrote about the following phases of psychological development:

1. *autistic phase:* 1 to 2 months, oblivious to anything except his or her needs;
2. *symbiotic phase:* 3 to 10 months, views others as an extension of himself; and
3. *separation–individuation phase:* 10 months to 3 years, gradually the child learns to differentiate and separate from others and begins to establish her identity.

Ten years after Mahler and coworkers outlined these concepts, Kernberg (1985) expanded them to develop his theory of borderline personality as follows:

1. During the separation–individuation phase, as just described, the child organizes experiences as only good or bad. This is splitting at the normal developmental level and is the primary organizing principle until this phase is completed.
2. Gradually the child is able to see others and self as partially good and bad, which enables him to integrate polarities.
3. The borderline condition occurs when, although the child has differentiated self from others, she has not integrated polarities and still sees things as all good or all bad; therefore, she is unable to tolerate ambivalence.
4. This condition was theoretically caused by an invalidating environment—specifically, a mother who was unable to allow the child's growing need for autonomy.

As you can see, splitting on this level is based on brain and personality development as well as on conditions in the environment. People whose personality is organized in this way typically see themselves, others, and the world in terms of black or white, good or bad. They often vacillate between the polarities, frequently even over the same object. Life often is riddled with chaos and deep depression.

I've found that working with clients who function with this level of ambivalence can be very confusing, as they seem to give extremely mixed messages. It helps to recognize the consistency in their full belief structure regardless of which belief is being expressed in the moment. For instance, *"I need you to nurture me, but I expect you to reject me so I need to distrust you."* This is the foundational belief system underlying the mixed messages.

You can see that this splitting exists on an *intrapersonal* level within their belief structure and on an *interpersonal* level as they communicate this extreme ambivalence in relationships. These patients have an intense need to believe that a person or therapist can meet the unmet needs they experienced as children. Toward this goal, they tend to start a relationship seeing the potential for these needs being met. They might idolize the person and see him or her as all good. Inevitably, however, the person is unable to meet all their needs perfectly. This failure, although a normal part of relationships, reinforces the other side of the coin, that is, the belief that no one will ever be able to meet their needs. The failure is met with a switch to seeing the person as all bad. This is consistent with Kernberg's (1985) theory that development was interrupted during the separation–individuation phase. Splitting also occurs when the patient sees one person as all good and portrays another as all bad. A common example in psychotherapy is when a client sees her new therapist as "perfect" and talks about the former therapist as having not understood, not truly listened, and so on. As the current therapist, we want to believe that we'll do a better job and may not recognize that the patient is splitting—and thus miss an opportunity for integration.

Avoidance

Procrastination, or avoidance, generally reflects ambivalence. When someone is avoiding making changes, it may be a result of normal or pathological ambivalence. Rather than think in terms of resistance, it is much more productive to help the client examine his reasons for avoidance or procrastination, educate him about the nature of ambivalence, and begin the process of resolving the ambivalence. People can be plagued by thoughts such as, "I really need to get that done" or "I forgot to do that again" or "I'll do it tomorrow." Until the ambivalence is resolved, the procrastination is likely to persist.

Denial

Denial is another potential indicator of ambivalence. As explained in the Stages of change model (Prochaska, DiClemente, & Norcross, 1994), people are unable to change until two things happen: They reach a certain level of motivation and have enough confidence that they have what it takes to make the change. The precontemplation phase is one of denial. Until a person has become aware for himself that there are risks involved by not changing, he is unlikely to begin the process. The person may be ambivalent about even beginning the conversation if he is not personally invested. When a client is expressing denial, it might be advantageous to ask if there is any small part of him that does see a need for change, so that the ambivalence can be harnessed as an agent of change. Another strategy would be to ask the client what percentage is committed to change and what percentage is fearful of change.

Suicidal Ideation or Gestures

One of the most important times to access ambivalence is when someone is having suicidal ideation or making gestures or attempts. Of course, this is probably the trickiest time as well, because every ideation or gesture must be taken seriously. When a patient expresses suicidal ideation, I generally explore the sources of hopelessness as well as the reasons the person hasn't acted on the thoughts. I also create, with my patient, a very detailed safety plan.

It can be incredibly difficult for a therapist to determine when suicidal gestures are a form of acting out, so to speak. I believe that most gestures, regardless of how serious or severe, have a communication embedded within them, an expression of fear, anger, or feeling misunderstood. When this is the case, it is important to address the communication and to help the patient find a more direct way to express feelings. Many therapists hesitate to do so because they don't want the patient to think that her therapist is accusing her of wanting attention or being manipulative. Therefore, addressing this must be done with skill and intentionality.

It's not necessary to determine whether a person is genuinely suicidal or looking for secondary gain, as long as both possibilities are carefully explored. If you explore both, you don't have to feel responsible for trying to decide which it is. Sometimes the patient doesn't know which it is. Additionally, even when people truly want to die, there is usually some form of communication or wish embedded in the impulse.

For example, Sarah was being treated for an eating disorder, depression, and anxiety. She had expressed suicidal ideation and had two suicide attempts in the past. She had developed a safety plan with her therapist and was in individual, group, and family therapy. She tended to be agreeable with suggestions, and, although fairly quiet, she participated in groups. She was usually smiling and seemed to hold in most of her negative feelings. But every once in a while, she would say something surprisingly sarcastic.

One day, Sarah's therapist received a call that Sarah was in the hospital after a suicide attempt. She was held for 2 days and released back into our care. Behind the closed doors of our treatment team, some staff members voiced their opinion that the suicide was a cry for attention, thus manipulative. Other members were concerned that she truly wanted to die because she had made several attempts and this one could have been lethal.

I consulted with Sarah on her first day back. I asked her about the day that she had hurt herself. She replied that she had been alone and just started feeling hopeless. I talked with her about her safety plan and about the steps that she had taken on the safety plan before the attempt. She had done several things, including telling her parents. She also said that she wasn't having any suicidal thoughts currently. As a team, we had come up with some changes to her treatment plan and a revised safety plan. Without determining whether Sarah had a wish to die or a wish to communicate, I simply said, "Sarah, sometimes when people are feeling so hopeless that they want to die, there is something that they want to communicate and just can't for some reason. Is there anything that you feel like someone just isn't getting on your team or at home?" She immediately, without the slightest pause, said her dad just didn't understand mental health problems. I reassured her that we would increase our attempts at helping him understand. Had I neglected to explore the hidden communication in her suicidal act, we wouldn't have known exactly where to focus our attention in ongoing sessions. This can be conceptualized as another dialectic such as, *I want to die* and *I want to be understood.* These two conditions do not seem capable of existing at the same time, yet they do. It isn't necessary to determine which is true; assume that both are.

Therapist Error

Finally, sometimes a person doesn't heed the advice of the therapist to work toward behavior change because of the therapist's mistake. Errors include lack of thorough assessment, lack of collaboration in goals, inadequate boundaries, lack of collaboration with others on the treatment team, and deficient skills or training in treating the problem area.

Pertaining to the topic of this book, an error can occur when a therapist voices one side of the ambivalence, which results in the patient's need to voice the other side with even more determination (as described earlier in the discussion about Tracy).

Another common error occurs when a therapist responds prematurely to expressions of fear that are coming from the patient's internal split such as, "I expect you to hurt me/I need you to nurture me." If the therapist is too quick to reassure the patient that she won't hurt her, the therapist is not addressing the fear, and this may hurt the person when the therapist can't be constantly available.

Probably the most common therapist error is when we as therapists want to believe everything a patient tells us. It can occur when the well-meaning therapist is siding with one side of a split, such as encouraging a person to end an unhealthy relationship when the therapist hasn't met the other person in the relationship, hasn't talked to the couples therapist, or hasn't fully assessed beliefs that the patient repeatedly projects in all relationships. In believing unconditionally what the patient says, we may unintentionally keep him stuck in personal narratives or beliefs that may be ruining his life.

In summary, it is important to identify expressions of ambivalence in psychotherapy so as not to make these common therapeutic errors. Ambivalence often is conceptualized as resistance, leaving the patient misunderstood and the ambivalence unresolved. When power struggles, manipulation, splitting, avoidance, and denial are experienced in psychotherapy, there is usually a wonderful opportunity to assess the likelihood that these are expressions of sincere ambivalence on the part of the client. The next chapter focuses on the treatment frame for identifying, understanding, and working with clients presenting with ambivalence.

Part II
Developing a Dialectical Framework for Recognizing Pathological Ambivalence

Chapter 4: A Dialectical Therapeutic Frame

Truth Is Paradoxical

A dialectic exists when two things that seem mutually exclusive are both true. The most common dialectic in psychotherapy is to want desperately to change yet be just as afraid to do so. When people don't understand the concept of dialectical reasoning, they are likely to get stuck in ambivalence. The primary focus in therapy with people stuck in pathological ambivalence, then, is to help them understand when something dialectical is creating the ambivalence and to refrain from taking on one side of the dialectic even if that side seems the most conducive to their therapeutic goals. This is not to say that it is never appropriate to make suggestions or give advice in therapy but that it is generally ineffective when dealing with pathological ambivalence.

Dialectics in this sense is defined as the reconciliation of opposites in a continual process of synthesis. Change is the result of a thesis interacting with its antithesis. One of the earliest philosophers to talk about dialectics in human development was George Hegel. He described (a) a beginning proposition called a thesis, (b) a negation of that thesis called the antithesis, and (c) a synthesis in which the two conflicting ideas are reconciled to form a new proposition (Schnitker & Emmons, 2013, p. 978). Hegelian dialectics suggests that in child development, the authority of the parents goes unchallenged in the early stages of a child's life. This complete obedience is our "thesis." As the child develops through adolescence, we typically see a phase of rebellion. The child must assert her own character and does this by rebelling against authority. Rebellion is our "antithesis." As the teenager matures into an adult, his attitude toward authority in general, and his parents or caregivers in particular, moderates. When independence is achieved, the individual no longer needs to rebel. Independence is our "synthesis"—I think this development corresponds to the development of child, adolescent, and adult ego states, as described in Chapter 2.

Having these opposing needs to accept and reject authority is natural, but under certain conditions, opposing needs may lead to pathological ambivalence. Linehan (1993) described difficulty managing dialectics as a cornerstone of developing borderline personality disorder that arises out of both a biological sensitivity and an invalidating environment. In dialectical thinking, all propositions contain their own oppositions; that is, truth is paradoxical. She outlined some of the common paradoxes in encountered in therapy:

- Need to change versus need to accept self
- Patient loses something she has versus getting her needs met in a new way
- Validating current views versus accepting a new viewpoint

To understand the amazing power of dialectics, consider the first step of Alcoholics Anonymous (AA). Once people in AA accept that they have no power over their alcoholism, they begin to have power. However, you can't begin to have power unless you have accepted that you are powerless. In some way, embracing these opposing truths must happen at the same time for change to occur. Another dialectic exists when considering who is responsible for change in a therapeutic relationship: the therapist or the client. I conceptualize this dialectically in that both are fully responsible for the change. A similar dialectic involves the artistic maneuvering of the therapist out of power struggles. When a therapist conveys to the patient that she really has no power to make the patient change, the therapist acquires power to enable the patient to change.

The Hot Potato Metaphor

Dealing with ambivalence in psychotherapy is much like holding the proverbial "hot potato." If you are not effectively dealing with the ambivalence, you may get burned (i.e., burned out). Imagine a person holding two potatoes, one in each hand. The two potatoes represent two sides of any dilemma that are currently being experienced. By way of example, suppose that one potato is labeled "have hope," and the other is labeled "give up." If you as her therapist try to encourage hope, the patient may be reminded of why she fears hope. It is as if the "have hope" potato begins to heat up. Hope is *hot* to the extent that it feels dangerous in some way. The client will want to get rid of the hot potato, so she might toss it to you. Because wanting her to have hope doesn't feel hot to you, you may be too willing to hold it for your clients. At the same time, if you hold the hope for her, she doesn't have to feel it and is left just holding her thoughts about giving up.

However, if your client is expressing her reasons to give up and you say something like "I hear that you have lots of reasons to fear hope," she may then start being afraid that she will never change. Now the "give up" potato starts to heat up. Having no hope starts to bring about its own set of fears. When a dialectic is operating and the patient lets go of the hot potato, there is initial relief. However, in the case of pathological ambivalence, the other potato will start to heat up in that it has its own set of fears. Other common dialects experienced by clients with pathological ambivalence are as follows:

> *"I want to be loved." If there is fear about rejection, this grows hot and may lead to "I don't need love."*

> *"No one will ever love me," combined with fear, might lead to "I must force you to love me."*

> *"I can't accept myself," accompanied by the belief that she's unacceptable, could then lead to intense anger whenever someone tries to give constructive feedback.*

Instead of inadvertently taking one potato from the patient, the therapist can help by using strategies that enable the patient to hold both potatoes simultaneously. In this way, neither gets too hot.

A client will toss the hot potato when she doesn't understand that dialectics exist and can be accepted as part of a complex truth (that she is allowed to have both). When we simplify truth into all-or-nothing beliefs, we often only capture portions of the truth, such as, *"No one will ever love me"* yet *"I need to be loved."* The following statements are indicative of a tossed potato

Dependent statements:
1. I know you were mad at me.
2. What do you think I should do?
3. Do you think what I did was wrong?

All-or-nothing statements:
1. I'm not good at anything.
2. It was all my fault.
3. You're the best (or worst) therapist I've ever had.
4. It wasn't my fault at all.
5. No one will ever love me.

Oppositional statements:
1. This might help others, but it isn't helping me.
2. You can't possibly help me, you've never been through this.
3. You have to say that, you're a therapist.

Patients describe this continuous alternating between opposing needs as feeling like there are two people in their heads or that they are going crazy. By learning to hold both at the same time and examining the fears and wisdom in each side, they will be able to begin resolving the ambivalence instead of bouncing back and forth. If the therapist makes a statement such as "so you feel both x and y" the client can experience holding both at the same time, which conceptually evens the heat between the two. Both potatoes become neither hot (fearful) nor cold (subconscious), but each are warm, indicating truth and fallacy on both sides. This also enables the client to recognize that the ambivalence is causing her discomfort—even suffering—and that it is her problem to resolve, not the therapist's. As a result, the therapist can feel more relaxed, which enables the patient to grow. When helping people hold both sides of any dilemma, you are working from a dialectical therapeutic frame.

As the therapist, it also is important to maintain the dialectic of expecting that the patient can make tremendous change, while simultaneously expecting that change of any kind is very difficult to achieve. It's not "either–or" but "both–and." Milton Erickson (e.g., Erickson, Rossi, & Rossi, 1976), often referred to as the father of hypnosis, developed the *Confusion Technique* to increase suggestibility in his patients. He would weave between seemingly disparate suggestions, saying things such as, "You are so ready to change and so tired of being in this situation, and you have so many reasons that you don't want to change, while you are confident that change is going to happen, and you have so little hope." Notice that he uses conflicting concepts such as confidence and hopelessness. It may sound contradictory, and even a little crazy, but he is simply voicing two truths that exist within a patient at the same time. Erickson found that when patients felt a small measure of confusion, they were more open to thinking in new ways.

Respect the Resistance to Change

In this section, I review many factors that contribute to the difficulty inherent in producing change.

Brain Physiology and Structure

As described in more depth in Chapter 1, there are several factors related to brain functioning that present obstacles to change. For example, the type of connectivity between brain structures (such as the limbic system with the prefrontal lobes) can interfere with one's ability to achieve a state of mindfulness or to observe the mind, which is necessary to resolve ambivalence. Additionally, lower levels of the amount of serotonin in the brain may make it difficult to achieve the state of calm needed to contemplate change. Finally, the more often a person has repeated a thought, feeling, or behavior, the more it becomes ingrained, literally, in the neuronal structure of the brain.

Self-Fulfilling Prophecy

Not only is the brain hardwired to repeat what it has learned, this repetition becomes a self-fulling prophecy. The client has a need to repeat the painful past while conversely craving a different outcome. For example, if someone grew up with a distant father and felt unlovable, tragically, she or he will be drawn to others who are similarly distant. This is an ineffective and generally unconscious attempt to be lovable to someone *like* the father, looking for someone like him to serve as a substitute in getting one's early needs met. Coupled with the preformed belief that "I am not lovable," the relationship will be difficult at best.

In the seminal book *Women Who Love Too Much*, Robin Norwood (1985) described the phenomenon of women who find themselves in similar relationships with different men, such as a woman who divorces an alcoholic and then marries another one. She described *loving too much* as a pattern of thoughts and behavior certain women develop as a response to problems from childhood.

Fear on Both Sides of the Dilemma

In the hot potato metaphor described earlier, you may recall that the patient experiences fear and anxiety, regardless of whether he is working on change or resisting change. As he attempts to avoid fear related to one side of the dilemma, he will be met with the fear associated with the other side, thus swinging from one side to the other. Patients often get stuck as they seem to have nowhere to turn. If the therapist tries to work on just one side of the dilemma at a time rather than working on the dilemma itself, it is likely that the patient will feel frustrated as well.

For instance, Ashley talked in therapy about how she wanted to break up with her boyfriend. She would spend most of her session describing how he was not good for her because he said things that made her feel hurt and inadequate. Her therapist agreed with her perception that she would be better off if she broke up with him (you guessed it, without having ever met the scoundrel). At the end of several sessions, Ashley would decide to break up and even made plans as to how to carry it out. The therapist waited each week to find out how the breakup had gone, just to be told again that it had not happened.

Finally, the therapist confronted Ashley on her "resistance," and Ashley began to state, shamefully, the reasons that she couldn't break up. It is regrettable that she experienced shame for something that she wasn't yet able to do simply because she hadn't yet worked directly on her ambivalence.

As she spoke of the reasons that she couldn't break up with her boyfriend, the therapist learned more about the relationship and about some of the positive aspects. Now the therapist changed her mind about supporting her to break up and began asking Ashley if maybe she should stay with him. Predictably, Ashley would then change the subject back to talking about how he didn't treat her well. The therapist felt as though they were simply swinging back and forth and getting nowhere. Exactly!

In an attempt to avoid the fear on one side of the dilemma, Ashley would be thrown into the fear on the other. Contemplating breaking up with her boyfriend would highlight her fear of being alone and unloved, but the thought of staying with him would shift the focus to her fear of never being with someone who encouraged her. She was stuck in fear with nowhere to turn. The therapist unknowingly was participating in the swinging. If the therapist tried to join one side of the dilemma, it just pushed Ashley to the other. It is important to note that there is not a simple solution when someone is ambivalent regardless of how obvious the *healthy* path may seem.

It's well established that fear reduces the ability of the brain to use the frontal lobes because fear enables the person to prepare for fight or flight. Change can occur more rapidly if the client isn't mired in the fear of giving up one side of a dilemma. We must use our frontal lobes to be able to ponder, observe our thoughts and feelings, create new thought patterns, and choose action plans—all of which are necessary when attempting to change. Fear and anxiety slow down creative processes and solutions. If we can avoid taking a side, the patient is likely to feel more relaxed and thus more able to connect with his own wisdom.

Expect Great Change

Although change requires huge effort, it is also the case that people generally already have internal resources to make changes once the ambivalence is harnessed or resolved.

Internal Growth Potential

When a person is ambivalent, it's like two parts of the person are trying to grow but using opposite strategies, such as when one part is trying to protect the person from pain while the other part is trying to get a need met, such as the need for love. The good news is that as a client begins to understand his own ambivalence, change can occur rather quickly owing to everyone's innate growth potential. This growth potential includes wisdom for what needs to happen next to allow change to occur.

Like Norwood's concepts about women who love too much, Harville Hendrix (2005) describes the *Imago* as the imprint of the positive and negative qualities of early caregivers. He writes that these qualities are wired in early in life in our hind brain. According to his theory, when engaging romantic partners, we can seldom overcome the urge to choose someone who has characteristics of our early caregivers.

To illustrate this growth potential, let's return to Ashley's story. Ashley grew up with a distant and sometimes critical father. Because he was the one she tried most to please, she ended up feeling unlovable. Unfortunately, as an adult she was then drawn to others who were similarly distant and critical. Most would view Ashley's compulsion to be with these types of men as self-sabotaging behavior, and, of course, on one level this is true. But it is also true that she is subconsciously looking for a way to heal the messages she took in as a child. If she can convince someone who is interpersonally distant to see that she is lovable, she will have overcome! People who aren't distant and who show her attention won't carry the same importance for her because she learned to feel bad about herself in the context of a distant father; thus, she may have trouble trusting them. Looking for the wrong type of person is actually a growth potential operating in her for healing of her original assumptions. And incidentally, the partner is drawn to her for similar reasons, so that if the two grow together, it can actually be more healing than finding a different type of person.

At the same time, however, there is another part of Ashley that is unhappy in her choice of partners, wanting something better for herself—another growth potential with an opposing goal. To resolve this dilemma, she will need to face the reasons behind her choice in partners and reevaluate the messages she took in as a child. Challenging these internal messages is a more powerful therapeutic strategy than focusing externally on changing partners.

Wisdom on Both Sides of the Dilemma

When people have ambivalence, there is not only fear on both sides but almost always some wisdom on both sides as well. This wisdom must be addressed before the course of action is likely to be successfully executed. In Ashley's situation, the wisdom could be addressed by stating, "You feel confused because you aren't ready to break up with him because he helps you believe that you are lovable, even though he also does some things which hurt your feelings." This is active listening in Carkhuff style (see Chapter 6). By pondering this statement, Ashley isn't forcing herself to choose immediately, so she may be able to look at her ambivalence in a new light. She might realize that if she heals her old belief, then his insensitive remarks won't hurt as much and she might choose to stay with him. Conversely, she might decide that if she changes her old belief, she won't be as afraid to leave the relationship. As a therapist, it isn't really our job to decide which path she takes. If you expect that your clients have wisdom within, your task becomes much more about helping them understand the wisdom and fallacy on both sides of the dilemma than about showing them how to make changes or which change to make. Thank goodness we don't have to feel responsible for this because we generally can't go home with our clients and meet the other people in their lives and determine with any certainty whether the relationship is healthy or unhealthy. One of my favorite quotes by Alexandra K. Trenfor is this: "The best teachers show you where to look but don't tell you what to see" (Kishor, 2015, p. 116). I think this applies to psychotherapists especially well.

Dysfunctional Narratives Can Be Rewritten

Finally, in expecting great change, we need to realize that change often occurs by gaining the awareness of the story a person tells herself, which began in childhood and which is producing ambivalence. The challenge is that when we are on automatic pilot (brain functioning according to previous experience), our story becomes a self-fulfilling prophecy. Fortunately, because of the brain's plasticity (it's always changing and rewiring), the "story" can be rewritten, although it takes conscious awareness and great effort. Specific strategies for helping clients rewrite their stories are presented in Chapter 7.

Common Pitfalls to Avoid With Pathological Ambivalence

The therapist will need to develop skills in sidestepping the projections (discussed later in the chapter) that are part of the story the patient tells herself. If a patient is convinced that others won't love her, then, of course, the only reason that you care is because she pays you to care. In this way, even the therapeutic relationship has potential to, at best, become a self-fulfilling prophecy and, at worst, become retraumatizing to the patient. This is not a reason to discontinue therapy.

All of the person's relationships have this potential, but the therapist needs to develop skills to minimize the injury. Unless a therapist is mindful of the dialectical nature of pathological ambivalence, common mistakes are likely to occur. The following pitfalls are some of the most common. Once you are aware of them, you can learn to sidestep these pitfalls with greater ease.

Working With Only One Side of Ambivalence at a Time

This pitfall is common precisely because clients often only express one side of their ambivalence. Ashley, for example, repeatedly stated that she needed to break up with her boyfriend. When helping people hold both sides of any dilemma, you are working from a dialectical therapeutic frame. See the section in Chapter 6 titled "Integrating Splits—While Staying Out of Them" for strategies to help bring both sides of the ambivalence into the room at the same time.

Falling Into a Split or Taking a Side

Although therapists are usually skilled in empathy and validation skills, we need to avoid taking sides and validating patients' distortions or projections because such behavior can leave patients stuck in personal narratives or beliefs that may be ruining their lives. Suffice it to say that if the patients' perspectives were always accurate, they probably wouldn't need to be in therapy. Valuable therapy time is wasted when we follow a patient down a well-worn path of blaming others rather than empowering the patient to shift his thinking or perspective to be more effective. Although it goes without saying that our patients have probably been hurt by others, once the pain has been experienced it becomes the "property," so to speak, of the one that felt it. Thus, it is theirs to manage and ultimately heal. I often tell my patients that if they want to blame others, they have every right to do so, but I want something even better for them, and that is that they focus on themselves and what they need rather than give that power to anyone else.

The first counseling split that I fell into happened when I was working as a youth director in a church. I was 22 and had a bachelor's degree in psychology. A young girl in my group would talk to me about her mother and I would be very compassionate and make statements like "she shouldn't say things like that to you," for example. This girl would then, of course, go tell her mother what I said. Her attendance started dropping off at youth group functions, and I sensed some angry stares from the mother in church services. I was too young and inexperienced to understand what was happening. In my naïve mind, her mother would just be thankful that I was taking time to be with her daughter.

After leaving the job and going into my master's program, this situation continued to bother me, and I took the opportunity to explore it in a class exercise practicing the empty chair technique. I played myself and then switched chairs and took on the role of the mom. In this role, I started saying things such as, "At 22 years of age, you judged my parenting—do you know how insulting that is?" "My daughter is fairly volatile and can exaggerate; did you ever think that she might have been exaggerating to get your sympathy?" "Did you ever come to me with your concerns?" "Your *compassion* actually made my job as a mother more difficult."

I was flabbergasted at the things coming out of my mouth. Apparently, on some level, I may have sensed some of these things, but I hadn't been aware of it until using this technique. I had royally fallen into a split. Of course, teenagers don't feel understood by their parents, and this is, to some extent, normal. And, of course, parents make mistakes (this mom wasn't very outwardly affectionate), but my offering empathy to the daughter had not helped the situation at all. Unless we are prepared to help a child separate from a parent, falling into a split just widens the split and has the potential for making things worse for the people involved. I consider it a rule of thumb that when there is any kind of split, whether interpersonal or intrapersonal, there is some wisdom on both sides, and the greatest wisdom is usually about halfway between the two. Therefore, effective interventions should be aimed at bringing the two sides closer together.

A common split is when a client tells you how his last therapist didn't understand him the way you do (putting you on the pedestal). Although this may be true and is certainly nice to hear, you don't want to fall into the split by *assuming* that it is true. To sidestep the split, you can say something like, "Being understood is important to you, and I'm glad that you feel understood. What things are you doing that are helping me understand you?" "Have there been any moments when you felt less understood with me as well?" And, finally, "It would be fine if you tell me when you think I'm not quite getting something." In doing this, instead of taking the role of the better therapist, you are conveying a message of openness. Furthermore, you don't have to be as worried about falling off the pedestal, since you already brought up the possibility that there could be times when you don't understand, and you have gently suggested that the power to be understood lies within him more than you.

To sidestep conversations with clients about someone else who is not in the room, I try to steer the conversation back to the person in the room. I might say something like "If she (a roommate for instance) were here, I would definitely want to talk with her about why she does that, but since it's just you and me here, let's talk about you." I also might ask questions such as, "How does her behavior affect your thoughts, feelings, behaviors or self-esteem? Does this remind you of other relationships you've had in the past?" It's my belief that if the client fully understands *herself* in this relationship, she'll know what she wants to do *about* the relationship.

Failing to Recognize When You Are Projecting

Everyone has baggage—even the best psychotherapists! We can't help but project our past experiences onto our clients and onto anyone else we meet. The first step to avoiding this pitfall is to know yourself and the beliefs that you will project, so that you can recognize when it's happening. I have a tendency project my belief that people expect me to be perfect, formed in childhood. Fortunately, this happens less pervasively than in my early career, but I still do it. When I'm making that projection, it is very hard to admit a mistake. If I go into detail, for example, to explain why I was running late to an appointment, I am projecting the message that people should be perfect. I also might get overly defensive when a client has a complaint.

Instead of attempting to be perfect, I can explain when running late that "I just couldn't get out of the house on time today, I'm so sorry. I wonder what it was like for you to have to wait for me?" Everyone has had trouble getting out of the house on time, and what's more important than my looking perfect is what it was like for the client. Once the focus is on your client, there's really no need for further explanation. I'm acutely aware of this possibility, and thus I've developed many strategies to avoid it, such as using mild, self-deprecating humor.

I've also learned that if I'm feeling defensive, then the client probably really needs me to understand where he is coming from. One example is when a client tells me that he doesn't think this therapy is helping. Rather than explain what he could do to make it work better, I've learned to pause and ask questions about his experience, such as, "That must be so discouraging, what do you think would be different if it were helping?" or "Do you have any feedback for me about what might work better?" or "Is there a specific goal you would like us to spend more time on?"

Finally, I remember hearing quite often in graduate school that we as therapists needed to be careful not to impose our values on our clients. Although I tried hard not to project my values, I think that I didn't truly understand the concept. I secretly believed that my values were all good, so it would be fine if I shared them in therapy.

I've come to believe that this concept is much broader than I realized. Even those values anyone would say they agree with could be hurtful when shared directly with a client. Here's an extreme example to make the point: I once worked with a woman who was in a relationship with a verbally abusive man. I very much wanted to share my value that no one should remain in that kind of relationship. However, I also knew that she had previously become suicidal whenever a relationship ended. If she was not yet ready to act on this value, she may have terminated counseling prematurely because of the shame she might experience in not being able to act on *my* value or, even worse, become suicidal. Thus, I chose instead to explore the beliefs formed in childhood. Her fear of being alone for the rest of her life was less tolerable than the verbal abuse that she experienced. Rather than impose my value, we worked instead on challenging the belief that she wasn't loveable.

Prematurely Challenging a Script

Although it's important to help our clients challenge their dysfunctional scripts or narratives, we first need to do a thorough assessment of the scripts (see Chapter 5). It can be especially confusing when working with someone who is struggling with pathological ambivalence, in that she may have contradictory scripts running at the same time.

Beth had developed dissociative identity disorder as a result of severe trauma in childhood. She lived alone and talked often about feeling very lonely. She expressed a desire to get a dog but seemed to continually procrastinate and make excuses to delay getting a dog. I thought a dog would be a fantastic idea for her. I thought it would be good for her to care for another living being and experience the affection that a dog would undoubtedly provide. One hesitation that she expressed was that she wouldn't be able to care for the dog. I believed that this was related to a general sense of worthlessness that she experienced (an old and pervasive script) and felt confident that she would be able to care for a dog.

I confess that I continued to press my agenda, feeling confused as to why she did not go ahead and get a dog. Eventually, and with some shame, she told me of having watched her father abuse one of their pets when she was growing up. She believed that she had a part of her that could be abusive to an animal. I felt such guilt that I had pushed my agenda without fully understanding the reasons for her "resistance to our treatment plan." I then asked her if she had any ideas of what could help. We had been working with her parts using the concept of a "committee meeting" to encourage integration. She determined that she could have a committee meeting with her parts to discuss the pros and cons of getting a pet. The next session, she related that there was one part of her that could keep the "aggressive" part of her from interacting with the dog, and she had already gotten a dog!

I think that my eagerness for Beth to have a dog had hindered her from exploring her ambivalence. Wanting to please me, she kept saying that she was going to get one but then procrastinated doing so. When I slowed down and asked her about it, she was able to pause and explore her own reasons. Only then was she able to get a dog and experience much joy and healing. The most powerful aspect of this endeavor occurred several weeks later when she related to me that the "aggressive" part of her had begun interacting with the dog appropriately. She explained that this part had been jealous of the other parts getting to play with the dog and was able to show them that she could be trusted not to hurt the dog. I believe this was tremendously healing for Beth and a sign that she was integrating parts in a similar fashion to how anyone integrates parts of their ambivalence.

Beth might have made faster progress if, when she first started making excuses for getting the dog, I had said something like this: "So, Beth, a part of you would like to have a dog but you haven't gotten it yet. Is there some part of you that doesn't want to have a dog?" It should be noted that this is the exact question I would use with someone who did not have dissociative identity disorder but was showing signs of ambivalence.

Personalizing Resistance

In his book *Resistance: Psychodynamic and Behavioral Approaches*, Paul Wachtel (1982) wrote: "Psychotherapy is no profession for someone who likes certainty, predictability, or a fairly constant sense that one knows what one is doing" (p. xiii).

Funny, right? And sometimes so true!

When a client is not progressing, it is very common for therapists to react with self-doubt. We want to be helpful; we're passionate about change, and no matter how experienced we are, we can still question our competence when working with certain individuals. I think that what is often termed negative transference is most likely to occur when clinicians succumb to power struggles with their patients and forget to understand the transference in light of the patient's projections.

Kinsey came to the Atlanta Center for Eating Disorders for intensive outpatient treatment for an eating disorder and major depression. She was assigned a therapist who had skill with both diagnoses. At first, she felt listened to and understood, but after a couple of sessions, she requested a change in therapists because they weren't "clicking." We know that not every patient clicks with every therapist, so as long as the patient is willing to have a wrap-up session with the first therapist, we honor the request to switch. The first therapist "debriefed" that she *knew* she had messed up somewhere but wasn't sure how, since Kinsey didn't give any specifics; she just had said that they didn't click.

Kinsey was assigned a new therapist with whom she "clicked" immediately. Things were going very well ... until they weren't. Kinsey complained that she didn't feel understood in the sessions. Kinsey also started making complaints about some of the group leaders that sounded like the complaints that she had with her therapist. The second therapist was doing everything she could think of to help Kinsey feel listened to and understood, yet was feeling ineffective. As the pattern emerged, we began to realize that Kinsey had a script related to her relationship with her mother. She talked about feeling as if her mother never listened and was very critical. Kinsey was able to see the pattern and recognize that whenever someone gave her suggestions or education, she heard it as criticism and felt misunderstood. Kinsey was primed to interpret many actions in this light. As she became more aware of this script, her therapist became more confident to help her see that her assumptions didn't apply in the present moment. Kinsey became empowered to rewrite the script that people wouldn't listen or understand her.

Becoming a target for a projection (vs. sidestepping the projection) can really hurt. Consider the projection as a dart aimed at you. Whether it is a complaint or a compliment, it still can be an expression of ambivalence and needs to be sidestepped. If you notice yourself experiencing negative emotions such as frustration, anxiety, irritation, or impatience with a patient consider if ambivalence is at play.

Taking Too Much or Too Little Responsibility for Change
One motto that I try to live by as a psychotherapist is: Never do something for the client that he can do for himself. As described earlier, if the client can interpret his own behavior, he doesn't need us to do that for him. My goal is to live by this motto in even the smallest ways. For instance, I enjoy the feeling of being helpful so much that I used to offer to look something up or write something down for the client. It is more empowering, albeit in a very subtle way, to just ask if they want to take it down or suggest that they Google it. Of course, if they didn't have a pen, I would supply one. Additionally, it can even be disrespectful to do something for someone when they are capable. "Here, let me do that for you" can send the message of "I'm better equipped to do this than you," especially with highly sensitive individuals.

This doesn't mean that I never do these kinds of things. If it's appropriate, I might offer to do something, but rather than jumping to do it, I'll say, "Would you like for me to do that for you?" As they consider the response to the question, they will be using their frontal lobes

Signs that a therapist is taking too much responsibility: Clifton Mitchell (2012, p. 2) listed the following signs that indicate a therapist has let resistance get the better of him:

- You feel like you are fighting or arguing with your client.
- You feel stressed and drained in an unhealthy manner after a session.
- You are working harder in your session than your client is.
- You are feeling burnt out with your work.

I would add the following:

- You dread the client coming or feel relieved when he or she cancels.
- You blame yourself for the client's lack of change.

Taking a step back to process this with the client might help get things moving in the right direction, such as, "I've noticed that I've been trying hard to convince you that you can change and we seem to get stuck when I do that."

Signs that the therapist is not taking enough responsibility: There also is a danger of not taking enough direction related to therapeutic process. For example:

- You feel as if you have little control over what happens in the session.
- You do not want to interrupt.
- Your client is spending the session storytelling about the previous week.
- You are getting sidetracked by the current crisis each week.
- You feel as if you are putting out fires.
- Your client is complaining about people who are not in the room.

Other signs that there may be an imbalance in who is taking responsibility for change include when the client is chronically late, puts you on a pedestal but isn't changing, or is making emergency phone calls between sessions. I'm not suggesting that every time one of these situations occurs it means that you are taking too much or too little of the responsibility; rather, consider this as one possible explanation in these circumstances.

Possible therapist interventions would be to begin the session by asking the client what was the highest and lowest point of the week (rather than just hearing about the week), and following up by exploring what made these moments the highest or lowest. Another approach could include processing the pattern, such as, "You have been going through so much recently! I have to ask you a question that may sound crazy: Is there any possibility that a small part of you finds something comfortable about having a crisis to talk about?" (Sometimes I follow with an example of a past client who doubted that people cared about her unless she was in crisis.) If your client is talking a lot about people who are not present in the room, you could intervene by stating something that puts more of the responsibility for change on the client. For example: "On one hand, you are very frustrated with your boss, but on the other, you haven't yet figured out what you can do to make things better."

Sidestepping Clients' Projections

Clients struggling with pathological ambivalence have beliefs, usually formed in childhood, about themselves, others, and their place in the world that contradict basic needs. These beliefs operate (often below the level of awareness) as a lens through which they see the world, guiding their interactions with others and their interpretations of events. These beliefs may be indiscriminately projected onto others or onto new situations. In therapy, these beliefs will also be projected onto the therapist or treatment team.

Carol grew up believing that she was "too much" for her parents and alternated between being ashamed of this and conversely feeling angry with them for not being able to handle her. She continually assumed, with shame, that her therapist also thought she was too much and simultaneously felt angry with her therapist. She vacillated between believing that she should never have any needs in therapy and feeling so needy that she made frequent emergency calls to the therapist. She felt angry at her therapist about what she *assumed* her therapist was thinking. The therapist attempted to reassure Carol that her fears were unfounded (even though a part of her was beginning to feel like working with Carol was becoming overwhelming).

Carol's therapist did not recognize the projection for what it was: a belief that needed healing before the dynamic could resolve. Once the therapist shifted the focus from their interpersonal dynamic, fruitlessly trying to reassure her, the dynamic within Carol could be explored. The therapist asked Carol if she felt this way often and in other relationships. Carol answered yes and talked about it beginning with her mother. Then, rather than continuing to attempt to reassure Carol, the therapist began saying, "You're feeling that old feeling again. What do you think that kid inside, who thinks she's too much, needs from *you* right now?" In this way, Carol turned her focus inside rather than projecting her fears on the therapist.

We therapists need to develop skills to sidestep the projections that are part of the story that patients tells themselves.

Avoid Answering Direct Questions

I sometimes use self-disclosure with my patients; however, I avoid answering direct questions when a projection is occurring. Lindsay suffered with depression and suicidal ideation. She placed an emergency phone call to me stating that she was suicidal. In our conversation, she was willing to contract for safety. In our next session, she came in looking defensive and somewhat angry.

Lindsay: Were you mad at me last night? I know you were.

The truth was that although I was more than willing to take her phone call, I also was frustrated at having been awakened. I am human. Lindsay was projecting onto me her expectation that people would not care about her while simultaneously needing to be dependent and therefore taken care of. My first inclination was to reassure her that I was not bothered by taking her phone call and that she was worthy of my time. Although this would have been comforting in the moment, she was unlikely to truly believe this because it conflicted with her narrative that people don't care about her. The other option would have been to say something authentic in an attempt to let her know that even though a small part of me was bothered, I was still more than willing to take the call. The likelihood is she would have only focused on the small part that was bothered and be wounded by that. I had a dilemma. Therefore, I sidestepped the dilemma as follows:

> **Therapist:** Hmm, before I respond to that, can I ask you a couple of questions?
>
> **Lindsay:** Okay.
>
> **Therapist:** What would it mean to you if I was mad about the phone call?
>
> **Lindsay:** It's okay because I'm used to it. I know I shouldn't bother you and should be able to take care of myself.
>
> **Therapist:** Is there any small part of you that would feel anything else?
>
> **Lindsay:** Well, it would seem just a little unfair because I was feeling really bad and thought I might hurt myself.
>
> **Therapist:** Okay, so you would both expect me to be mad and also feel that it was unfair. So, what would it have meant to you if I wasn't mad about the phone call?
>
> **Lindsay:** I'd be glad but I wouldn't necessarily believe you. No one likes getting awakened in the middle of the night, especially me.
>
> **Therapist:** If I were mad, would it remind you of things from the past?
>
> **Lindsay:** Sure. My mom always acted like I was too much for her. I'm used to it.
>
> **Therapist:** So you make the assumption (the projection) that I was mad, based on how you felt with your mom, and that's totally normal as long as you continue to believe the things that you told yourself back then. I would think this makes you really ambivalent when it comes to needing help or even connecting with people for that matter.

We then spent much of the session talking about times when she felt neglected by her mother. She recognized that she alternated between feeling shame and anger (just like she had with me). We explored the wisdom on both sides of her dilemma. We never got back to whether I had felt mad. It didn't matter anymore.

Teach Clients to Identify What's Needed From Self and Other

The preceding conversation with Lindsay went on to encourage her to identify what she would need from *herself* if I had been mad, and what she would need from *me* if I had been mad.

> **Therapist:** So, Lindsay, when someone is mad at you, what do you need to do for yourself?
>
> **Lindsay:** I don't know, I just want to make them stop being mad at me.
>
> **Therapist:** Of course, that would be nice, but I believe that you can't always make that happen or even if you can, there might be a part of you that wouldn't believe them.
>
> **Lindsay:** I probably need to remind myself that I can't be perfect, or that I'm doing the best I can. I could also validate that I had done nothing wrong, if that's the case.
>
> **Therapist:** I like that. Supporting yourself is helpful because only you can really know what your needs and intentions are.
>
> **Lindsay:** I always criticize myself when someone is mad at me, even if it's a misunderstanding.
>
> **Therapist:** When you wondered if I was mad at you, what could you have done for yourself?
>
> **Lindsay:** I could have told myself that it's okay to inconvenience someone if I am really in need.
>
> **Therapist:** That's a great resolution of your ambivalence of whether you should have called. Both can be true: that you are in need and someone might be inconvenienced. I believe it is okay to inconvenience someone a little if it helps you a lot. So, what do you need from a person if they are mad or inconvenienced?
>
> **Lindsay:** It would be nice to know that being mad at me doesn't mean that I'll be rejected.
>
> **Therapist:** How could you find out?
>
> **Lindsay:** I guess I could just ask if you still cared about me even though I had inconvenienced you.
>
> **Therapist:** When you ask a question like that, I think it is both strong and vulnerable, which is a nice combination to have in relationships. When you came in today, you seemed mad. I think it was because you were assuming that I would be mad and possibly reject you, so you were beating me to the punch. It's

great that you can just state that you need to know if I still care even if I was inconvenienced. That's really what you wanted to know and is much more important than whether I was mad.

Share Your Dilemma as a Therapist

When you feel ambivalent about how to respond to a client, it can be helpful to share both sides of your dilemma. You can then ask the client to choose the response that she prefers. This encourages the client to take responsibility for the course of the session *and* models how to deal with ambivalence. If you're torn about how to respond, it is likely that the client will be ambivalent as well, so that in responding to your dilemma, they will have to practice resolving ambivalence.

Kayla was a recovering alcoholic who also suffered with bulimia. She had been sober for 2 months. It has been our experience that people need more than 2 months' sobriety before taking on treatment for another major disorder, but she was adamant about wanting to begin treatment for her bulimia. We agreed to admit her to our program on the condition that she agree to return to substance abuse treatment if she relapsed. In individual treatment, she started off strong, applying the strengths that had enabled her recovery from alcohol to her eating disorder. However, it became more and more difficult for her to manage feelings that arose without relying on either alcohol or binge-eating. After one particularly difficult weekend, she succumbed to the urge to drink.

As Kayla described what had led up to her decision to drink, I was filled with two opposite emotional reactions. One was deep compassion for the disappointments that she had experienced over the weekend (she had felt betrayed by a person very close to her). The other was frustration and sadness that she had made such a self-sabotaging decision and jeopardized her eating disorder recovery. Both emotions were strong and in conflict with each other, and I didn't know how to proceed. It had taken her a long portion of the session to tell me what had happened, so there definitely was not time to process both (support and comfort) adequately. I couldn't decide which of my reactions to choose. Either way felt both right and wrong on some level. They were both true and possibly helpful reactions. I decided to ask her which she needed. I said, "Kayla, I have a dilemma right now. On the one hand, I'm truly sorry about what happened this weekend and am wondering if you need to talk through your feelings about how you were treated and how it brought up pain from other relationships, as well. But on the other hand, I want to 'bop you upside the head' for reacting the way you did [this was a phrase that she was fond of using and I knew that I could use it playfully as well] and for breaking our contract. Which do you need right now?"

Kayla paused for a moment and then courageously said, "I need you to bop me upside the head." I nodded and slightly frowned, communicating that I thought this was the wise choice but that it made me a little sad that we couldn't just talk through her disappointment. In this way, I think she felt very much like I was empathizing, but also supporting her wisdom for the choice she made. This was so much more rewarding for both of us than if I had just chosen to encourage her to talk about how she had felt mistreated and the pattern of this in her life *or* how she had made choices over the weekend that were self-sabotaging and planning a course of action. I had believed that the latter was the more appropriate choice but couldn't bring myself to make it for her because it seemed less empathic. Fortunately, by using this strategy of talking about my dilemma, I didn't have to make the choice. We spent the remainder of the session reviewing the choice points during the weekend and how she could have responded differently at each of them. We then made a plan for her to return for treatment of her alcoholism. She determined that her sobriety was not stable enough to handle the emotional vulnerability that she felt when she tried to give up her eating disorder. I felt confident, though, that the skills she had gained in her time with us would support her in her next phase of treatment.

Facilitate Combining Wisdom of Therapist and Client

As in the concept just described, I usually explain to my patients that we must combine our wisdom to be successful. I bring to the table my training, knowledge, and skills. The patient brings her own experiences, learning history, narratives, unique sensitivities, and talents. The best chance of successful intervention is in combining our wisdom about what is needed.

Without inviting clients to contribute their own wisdom, the therapist is less likely to be helpful. In the example with Beth's dog, she had wisdom unknown to me as to why it was not a good idea, and until she explained that to me, I was making a suggestion she was not yet able to follow.

Explain to the patient the concept of combining your wisdom early in the process, so that they can feel empowered to speak up when something doesn't sit right with them for any reason. This also helps the therapist to sidestep projections such as "my therapist is the one who has the answers and will save me," or, conversely, "my therapist just doesn't understand me," or even worse, "my therapist must think I'm weak and stupid since I don't do what's recommended."

Use Interpersonal Processing Strategies

Using the relationship that you have with your client is one of the most powerful interventions in avoiding problems in therapy caused by projections. Although this chapter focuses primarily on sidestepping projections, the therapist can use interpersonal processing techniques to intentionally and temporarily step right in front of a projection. Interpersonal processing therapy is based on three assumptions (Teyber, 1992):

1. We are relational in nature; thus, many problems are interpersonal in nature.
2. Familial experience is the central source for learning about ourselves.
3. The therapist–client relationship can help solve problems.

Many seasoned therapists use interpersonal processing effectively in their practices to reduce resistance. It can be especially helpful when the therapist and client have already assessed the types of beliefs that the client tends to project onto others. Through interpersonal processing, you can spot instances when these beliefs are being projected onto you and ask about them as they occur. When using interpersonal processing you need to be authentic. The client often knows in his gut if you are simply saying what you know he wants to hear.

The following is an example of how I implemented interpersonal processing with a young client.

Nicole seemed very sensitive to what I thought about her. She had felt rejected and misunderstood by her own mother growing up. It turns out that her mother was overwhelmed trying to raise six kids and relied extensively on Nicole, who was the oldest, to help with the younger siblings. My client wasn't actually rejected by her mother (although her needs were neglected), but this was her experience, and she developed a belief that others would use her and reject her. She was extremely dependent on me to reassure her that I cared about her and found her worthy of my time. The first phase of our relationship was spent building trust that I found her acceptable and worthy. When she seemed withdrawn in session, I would ask her to talk about what she was feeling, and she would often talk about feeling that I was judging her. Asking her what I was doing that was giving that message, and then reaffirming to her what I was actually thinking or feeling in the moment, was very helpful to her. A typical session with Nicole might proceed like this:

Therapist: You seem like you are distant, almost alone in your thoughts.

Nicole: Yes, I'm not in a very good mood.

Therapist: Has something happened in here with me that has affected your mood? (interpersonal processing question)

Nicole: Not, really, I just feel embarrassed.

Therapist: Can you tell me what you're feeling embarrassed about right now? *(This is the interpersonal strategy of bringing the feeling into the here and now.)*

Nicole: No, it's just a vague sense of being judged.

Therapist: See if you can identify which thoughts might be going through your mind right now that are causing you to feel that sense of being judged.

Nicole: Well, last week I think you were disappointed in me about the choices that I made.

Therapist: So you think I was disappointed, and that makes you feel like I'm judging you.

Nicole: Yes, and I know that it's probably not true, but I feel like you only want me to get better so you can feel like you're helpful.

Therapist: You feel like my wish for you to get better is about me rather than you. *(I put it this way knowing what her experiences taught her to believe in childhood about being used.)*

Nicole: Yes, I know it's stupid but I really do feel this way.

Therapist: Would you like to know what is going through my mind as you say these things?

Nicole: Yes, as long as you're not mad at me.

Therapist: If I were mad at you, that would seem intolerable at this point.

Nicole: *Nodding.*

Therapist: I can reassure you that right now I'm not feeling any anger at all. *(I'm trying to be very authentic by saying that I don't feel any anger right now. Although she would probably love for me to say that I would never feel anger toward her, I couldn't promise that, and she wouldn't believe it anyway, so I am careful to keep these statements in the present tense).*

Therapist: What I am feeling is a little sad and a little confused. Would you like to hear more about that?

Nicole: *Nodding.*

Therapist: I feel sad that you have been sitting here feeling rejected when I was actually feeling accepting toward you. You were in a bad mood because you were assuming that I was judging you last week. I admit that I felt saddened by some of your choices because I knew that they were going to hurt you in the long run. I may have even felt a little frustration. I'd like you to believe that the frustration I felt was in your behalf, though. Much bigger than the frustration from last week, though, was a feeling of admiration that you came to the session today even though you were afraid that I might feel mad at you and a respect for how hard these changes are going to be for you to make. Does what I'm saying ring true for you?

Nicole: I guess. It's hard to believe, but it does sort of make sense. I don't see you as a judgmental person.

Therapist: I'm glad to hear that, because I also mentioned that I felt confused. I was feeling confused about what I may be doing to make you feel like I'm mad or rejecting.

Nicole: Not anything, really, just a look in your eyes last week.

Therapist: Have I said anything that might help you interpret the look you saw last week in a new light? *(It's not necessary here to admit or deny the look, she saw something.)*

Nicole: Yes, I'm trying to. You said you were sad and maybe just a little frustrated.

Therapist: Maybe feeling rejected by me is related to those beliefs that we talked about earlier that you learned as a child. It is good for you to tell me anytime I do something that triggers those beliefs so that we can both examine what's happening right away. Do you feel like you can do that?

Nicole: *Nodding.*

In this exchange, I encouraged Nicole to give words to her feelings and to process those feelings in the context of our relationship. Although I hadn't initially known that her feelings were about me, this strategy seeks to bring feelings into the moment and to query how they might apply to the therapeutic relationship. I openly discussed how I was feeling toward her to help her reevaluate her interpretations. However, even though I intentionally stepped in front of her projection, I was committed to stepping out of it as quickly as possible to help her broaden the perspective to see beyond our relationship. I followed up the interpersonal processing strategy by connecting her current feelings to beliefs that she formed in childhood to help her become more aware of how she projects those onto new relationships. We would then move on to working to develop new beliefs based on new experiences. After processing what a client is feeling within the therapeutic relationship, it is important to then to broaden the focus as follows.

Therapist: Do you see anything different between the look you noticed from me last week and the way you felt when you saw that kind of look from your mom?

Nicole: Yes, I never felt like her frustration was on behalf of me.

Therapist: So your interpretation of my look was in light of how you felt as a child. Do you think you interpret others' reactions to you in this way as well? *(Here I'm broadening the perspective beyond the therapy experience.)*

Nicole: I'm sure I do.

Therapist: So, what would you need to say to yourself or do for yourself when you start to feel judged or used? *(At this point my attempt is to help her move from a dependent, victim stance to one of empowerment.)*

Nicole: I could ask myself to consider that I'm projecting.

Therapist: That would be great! But suppose it is the worst-case scenario and the person really is attempting to take advantage of you? You know that sometimes happens to all of us. What could you do for yourself in that situation?

Nicole: Ask myself if I want to do whatever is being asked, and, if not, recognize that I get to choose what I do and who I want to be in a relationship with.

Therapist: And how could you interpret what is happening in a new way?

Nicole: That it doesn't reflect on my worth.

Nicole and I spent several sessions on the last three questions. Achieving this insight in the session is just the beginning of facilitating behavioral change. The client will also need to learn how to recognize when the projections are happening outside of the therapy sessions, which is often quite difficult.

In a different situation, I overused this technique. I knew that Lori had a problematic relationship with her mother and that she often projected her insecurities onto others. As she was talking about a coworker with whom she was having difficulties, I asked her if she ever felt the same way with me. Having been trained to bring the focus on the here and now, I thought this was a brilliant query. Apparently, I had asked this more than once and possibly at ill-placed moments, as on this day. Her response to me was, "It isn't always f'ing about you!" Talk about a moment when you wish the ground would just part and swallow you up. I was mortified. So, I simply said, "You are so right. I was using a technique that I learned in school without actually considering if it was appropriate right now and I apologize." Later we both got a kick out of that moment, but it had been pretty awful for me.

My mistake in this situation was not waiting to see whether I could help Lori process her projections in the context of the relationship with her coworker first. I basically interrupted her as she talked about her coworker to, in effect, make it about me. This actually made her feel that I wasn't validating her and that I was siding with the coworker. The exchange would have been more effective had it gone like this:

Lori: She (coworker) always acts like she's too busy to talk except when she wants to brag about something. She ignores me when she comes in to work sometimes. When she does want to talk, it's always about her wonderful husband and kids. I never feel like I have anything important to say. *(I knew enough about Lori's history to know that this is how she felt around her mom.)*

Therapist: Do you think it would be helpful to share with her how it makes you feel?

Lori: Hmm, maybe, but I really don't know if I care about her enough to want to be that vulnerable.

Therapist: Yet you're talking about it here, so it must be important to you on some level. What do you feel when she's doing these things?

Lori: I don't know, kind of small. Inadequate and awkward, I guess.

Therapist: Do you feel those feelings often, or is it just with this person?

Lori: I guess I feel that way a lot. It's a lot like how I felt with my mom. *(This is where I made the interpersonal query in the actual conversation. Instead, I could have said …)*

Therapist: Yes, that reminds me of the way you felt growing up. Like the beliefs that you identified feeling when you were growing up? You checked off the belief that "I'm not as competent and important as others." That's very similar to how you're feeling now.

Lori: I see that, but she is really rude. *(I like this response because she's sounding less like a victim.)*

Therapist: I'm not saying that she isn't doing the things that you are talking about, and it does sound rude. But my concern is how much power you give her over your feelings. If she were here, maybe I'd be helping her with interpersonal skills. But with you, I'm much more interested in how you allow her to make you feel. *(This statement empowers her to realize that she chooses her reaction to others, even if subconsciously.)* You react by feeling inadequate. Is there any other way that you could interpret the situation?

Lori: Well, maybe she does all the talking because I can never think of anything to say.

Therapist: So it may not be that she thinks less of you. Would it be okay if we spent some time exploring how what you felt as a child is affecting how you react currently?

Interpersonal processing of the moment can be helpful but should be used sparingly, and only if you can't create the same outcome otherwise. Before using interpersonal processing strategies, I am clear as to why I'm choosing to do it at the time and then get the focus off me as soon as possible, so that it returns to the patient and her relationships. Otherwise, the patient may develop undue dependency on the therapist, give undue credit to the therapist for changes made, and, worst of all, lose hope of developing supportive relationships outside of therapy.

In my experience, the best times to use interpersonal processing strategies are the following:

1. If you sense that the patient is feeling something specifically about you but is not clearly stating it, such as in the case with Nicole at the beginning of this section.
2. Early in the therapeutic process to build trust. This should occur after identifying the projections that the client is likely to make and only when it seems apparent that these beliefs are being projected.
3. When a client has a pattern of difficulty in interpersonal relationships that can best be explored in the context of the therapeutic relationship.

It is not necessary to use interpersonal processing statements when the client can process the projections in the context of the external relationships or when the same goals can be achieved through working with ego states, such as inner child (see Chapter 6).

Going With the Resistance

Another way to therapeutically address the dialectic of both wanting to change and fearing change is to *go with* the resistance. Going with the resistance occurs whenever you temporarily let go of the agenda to understand or validate the client's fear of change. Effective therapy with ambivalent clients always involves using strategies to go with the resistance. Therapists are sometimes hesitant to lean into the resistance for fear that the patient will interpret the behavior as permission not to change. But actually, this strategy often helps patients feel fully understood. As discussed previously, when you spend time showing the patient that you want to understand why it's hard to change, there is less need for her to resist.

Empathy and Validation

One of the most common ways of going with resistance, although often not recognized as such, is simply making empathic statements to the client about her struggle. For instance, Joanie was battling depression and social avoidance. After spending the better part of an entire session preparing for an upcoming event, she told me in the next session that she hadn't been able to make herself go. She had begun to think about how she wouldn't know what to talk about (something that we had thoroughly planned for) and had become too anxious.

Part of me wanted to talk about the potential consequences of continuing on the path of social isolation and how exposure was the best way to reduce her fear, but I chose to begin with empathy. I said that I knew she must have been feeling really bad and asked if she'd tell me more about it. This conversation led to learning more about the criticism she endured as a child about her shyness.

Paradoxical Interventions

Paradoxical interventions are much more provocative strategies for going with resistance and are used to suggest the opposite behavior than what you are attempting to achieve. The key with paradoxical interventions is to use them sparingly. Suggest them only when other interventions have failed and you believe that what you're suggesting is true and not just a trick. A technique called *Prescribing the Symptom*, in which a symptom or problem behavior is planned to occur, creates a different set of contingencies than if the behavior occured as the result of an irresistible impulse. For example, a person who compulsively vacuums could be given a prescription to vacuum for 2 hours rather than her habit of vacuuming for 30 minutes several times a day. This is similar to exposure with response prevention, which is sometimes used to treat bingeing and purging. The patient is told to engage in a binge at a certain time with a prearranged way of blocking the purge. Journaling during this experience can heighten awareness of the functions of the behavior.

Craig had a cocaine addiction. He had been married for 8 years and had started his own business. He initially had been doing well financially and interpersonally. However, the deeper he got into his addiction, the more he squandered the couple's savings, bringing them to the brink of bankruptcy and almost losing his business. After a couple of DUIs and a short stint in jail, he was mandated to go to therapy. He requested that his wife be involved because of her intense fear that he would return to using cocaine. When I met Craig and his wife, he had been clean for 6 months, was faithfully attending AA, and was successfully rebuilding his business. However, his wife was miserable, and she was making him miserable through her constant fears that he would relapse. She managed all the finances, called him incessantly to see what he was doing, questioned him constantly at home, and put him on a strict allowance where he had to account for every dime he spent. Everyone advised her to stop complaining and questioning him, fearing that she was going to drive him back to using. She desperately wanted to change her behavior as well, but her extreme anxiety prevented her from doing so. She reported that she knew that Craig was doing everything that he was supposed to, but she just couldn't let go of her need to control him.

During our first couple of sessions, I, like the others in her life, focused on helping her shift her behavior, such as limiting the number of times she called him at work. She was unable to change any of the anxiety-driven behaviors. On our third or fourth session, Craig was late, and I spent a few minutes alone with her. She began talking again about how she had not accomplished anything that we had talked about and was feeling hopeless. It then occurred to me that as long as everyone around her focused on the changes she needed to make before she was ready, the more anxious she felt, which only served to increase the checking behaviors. I realized that I would need to try something drastically different.

I admitted to her that I realized that I had been going about this completely wrong. I confirmed that anyone would feel anxious in her situation and that she had a certain amount of anxiety that she was going to have to feel and address. The more she tried to avoid experiencing and processing her anxiety, the longer it would take her to get through it. I advised her that it would probably be better to worry *more* until she was done. Aware that she had come to me to help her worry less, I was concerned that she might get up and leave my office. Instead, she burst into tears, telling me that finally she felt understood.

I recommended that we come up with a plan for increasing worry to make up for all the effort that we had put into trying to stop the worry prematurely. So we came up with a paradoxical intervention. Just then, her husband arrived, and with my heart beating slightly faster, I explained the plan to him. I suggested that she save up all her worry thoughts until he came home from work and then talk about them for no less than 45 minutes. They were to set a timer for 45 minutes and when it rang, they would be finished until the next night. His job was to sit and listen patiently to every worry thought that she had experienced and answer any questions that she had. I reiterated how important it was to do the full 45 minutes if they wanted the worry to ever lessen.

I held my breath, assuming again that he would think my suggestion was crazy and walk out. Instead, after a short pause, he said, "Well, that's much better than what we've been doing." The following week, they told me that they had tried really hard to use the whole 45 minutes but usually didn't last more than about 20. I suggested that they try even harder the next week, for fear that all the worry wasn't being expressed. By the next session, they had completely stopped and she had spontaneously been able to change some of the behaviors that we had been working on. I saw her laugh for the first time in this session.

I used this paradoxical intervention because I truly believed that even though the treatment goal was to decrease her worry, she needed to fully allow herself to worry until she was "worried out," so to speak. I believed that directly challenging the worry was adding to it and thus prolonging the attempt to get through it. Additionally, by saving all her worry thoughts so that they didn't get watered down during the day, Craig's wife learned that she could compartmentalize the thoughts, which gave her more control over them. Finally, by prescribing an ordeal, I set up a contingency in which she had the freedom to worry less than advised.

With individuals who are suffering with pathological ambivalence, there is a part of them that fears change so deeply that it can be helpful to align with that part by suggesting that the person change very slowly. Although some problems have to be addressed quickly because, for instance, they have medical consequences, this tactic can be effective with many types of problems.

Asking clients why they want to change when the problem behavior is functioning so well, enables them to access their own desire for change rather that resisting your hope for their change. It may seem strange because the patient is actually the one who sought you out, but this is a common experience with people who struggle with pathological ambivalence. The timing of this question is important. It works best when the client is already voicing reasons for not changing.

For example, Christine was struggling with anorexia nervosa and had identified many functions that her anorexia was serving. She had been overweight as a child, and her anorexia provided her with much relief from being teased for being fat. She knew that focusing on her weight allowed her to avoid the emotions that she felt about herself, which generally centered on shame. She also knew that controlling her food intake made her feel strong and competent. As she talked about these functions, I wanted to point out how her anorexia was also killing her, which would have been an accurate, but ineffective, statement at the moment. Instead, I gently said, "I see how important it has been for you and how scary it would be to change it now. Given all that, I wonder what even makes you consider recovery?" I said this with sincerity because I truly wondered this, given how effective the anorexia was in preventing such pain. However, this was not what she expected me to say at the moment, and I watched as her resistance melted away. She didn't need to convince me of how important her anorexia was, since I communicated to her that I understood. She was then able to contemplate, in the same space of time, both why she wanted recovery and why recovery would be difficult.

Sometimes therapists are wary of making statements like this for fear that it will romanticize the dysfunction or will slow down the process. But I find the opposite to be true. Once the client feels completely understood, change can occur more rapidly. It is as if I jump over to the side of the resistance temporarily to understand their experience, knowing that I will return to the side of change later.

Another way to avoid or disengage from a power struggle is to predict failure of a proposed strategy. The therapist might say something like, "I have an idea, but I don't think you can do it yet." In this type of situation, the therapist is taking the voice of resistance possibly eliciting the part of the person that desires recovery. If the therapist has already engaged in a power struggle such as trying to encourage change or hope that is being met with resistance, he or she can shrug and say something like, "You're right, you're not yet in a place to feel the hope that I feel for you." It would be helpful to follow this up with a strategy aimed at exploring the function of the problematic behavior. A gentler approach to predicting failure is simply talking about the fact that change is not a straight line but sometimes will be two steps forward and three steps back. It can be helpful to explain this so that patients don't assume that change is impossible.

In summary, whenever I realize that I've let myself take on a projection or engaged in a power struggle around change, I think of the scenes from *Ghostbusters* movies when the characters tried to avoid being "slimed" by the ghosts. The strategies in this chapter may enable you to quickly jump out of the way of the ghost, so to speak, so that you don't become the target of the projection, while simultaneously remaining in close proximity to your client. If the patient is able to see the consistency in the thoughts and feelings that she is projecting, she may be ready to start rewriting the narrative that she formed in childhood.

Three Stages of Treatment

Although pathological ambivalence is often what motivates a patient to come into therapy, its expression may result in slowing or even halting the therapeutic process. Consequently, therapists benefit from learning specific skills to help their clients navigate the ambivalence with the goal of integrating or resolving it. This endeavor is enhanced by remembering what we want to convey to our clients: We are *on* their side without *taking* a side. The last part of this book is devoted to treatment strategies for harnessing and moving through pathological ambivalence. Generally speaking, I recommend three broad stages for resolving ambivalence.

Stage 1: Assessing Schema and Narrative

When people are struggling with pathological ambivalence, it is first necessary to set up mutual goals via thorough assessment. An initial step usually involves listening, and therefore witnessing and validating any formative experiences the patient is ready to discuss. A complete history needs to be taken. The patient needs to have his story fully witnessed at least once in his life, and he needs eventually to know that his feelings and behaviors make sense. The focus of the assessment phase is on the past and on building rapport. However, it is important to spend minimal time on this endeavor, especially if the patient has told his story in previous therapeutic endeavors. Otherwise, the patient may get into the rut of spending most of his therapy time talking about how others, either in the past or present, have done him wrong and the caring and well-meaning therapist could unwittingly reinforce this behavior by allowing it to continue.

The second primary focus of this stage is to assess the schemas, narratives, and scripts that a person has developed and are producing the ambivalence. It also is helpful to assess problematic behaviors that result from the scripts, the function of these behaviors, and the patient's level of motivation. The therapist likely will need to provide a lot of education regarding the factors involved in developing ambivalence. Also involved will be clarifying goals, planning treatment, and obtaining informed consent.

Stage 2: Moving Through Ambivalence

The second stage addresses resolving pathological resistance. Although information from the past often emerges in these techniques, the focus is on the present in a practical, objective, and nonevaluative manner. During this stage, the patient learns to be mindful of current thought patterns, behavioral triggers, and choice points. The patient is taught fundamental skills for understanding and resolving ambivalence.

Stage 3: Rewriting Dysfunctional Narratives

The third stage is devoted to rewriting the cognitive scripts or narratives from an adult perspective. As you read in Chapter 2, many psychological perspectives incorporate into their theories of human health and pathology a focus on narrative, script, or schema. In general terms, during the developmental years of childhood, a person will form beliefs about how the world works and about her place in the world. These beliefs will be affected by temperament, experience, brain functioning, and brain development. If pathological ambivalence has developed, these beliefs will have to be reevaluated and replaced.

Part III

Treatment Strategies for Pathological Ambivalence

Chapter 5: Setting the Stage for Change

A Therapeutic Roadmap

The following treatment strategies are grouped according to specific therapeutic goals and can be conceptualized loosely as being used in therapy in the order presented in this book. Of course, this is a conceptualization or road map to help you know where you're headed and why. In practice, therapy usually involves a journey that would look more like a spiral than a straight line.

Primary Goals for the Therapist

Be Aware of Your Own Agendas

Similar to being aware of projecting our values, we need to monitor our own agendas. One of our primary agendas as a therapist is to help people change. However, if this agenda is too much about you, a person with pathological ambivalence may become even more resistant to change. Out of fear, these patients hold on to schemas and behaviors that, although dysfunctional, *feel* necessary. If you focus your energy on trying to pry them loose because you have an agenda focused on outcome, then it may actually feel to the client that you are being insensitive—or even worse, simply caring about your own success.

The challenge is to communicate *both* goals: that you sincerely care about your client's healing *and* that you are somewhat indifferent toward outcome—another dialectic. In some ways, both are true, but you will communicate it differently depending on the topic. Being indifferent sounds harsh, but it's all about timing. When focused on what is currently happening in the client's life regarding her change attempts and difficulties making changes, I am fully engaged. As I listen to the client talk, I sincerely communicate that she is most important to me in that moment. I communicate verbally and nonverbally that the client is fascinating, beautiful, and fabulous in her unique way. I want her to believe that there is no place I'd rather be than with her in this moment.

At the same time, I communicate something akin to indifference when talking about outcomes. It is a message of neutrality that can be empowering. I might say something like, "What you choose to do with your future is up to you," or "You hired me to help you, but at any time, you can fire me." Another way that I communicate neutrality is when suggesting a higher level of care. I might say, "Here are your options, and my decision to continue working with you will be based on these factors, but it's totally up to you which path you take; only you truly know which is possible or best for you." By dispassionately respecting his choice to choose, there is no need for a power struggle. This frees the patient to explore his reasons for wanting to change as well as his fears of changing.

If the therapist has expressed enough sincere caring when focusing on the present moment, the client generally feels relieved that the therapist is not emotionally invested in making her change, but is invested in her as a person. This concept is related to knowing when to take control and when to let go, or the dialectic of accepting the client as she is while encouraging change. I am constantly weaving between stances of caring and indifference. There is a kind of energy shift that I experience as I navigate between caring and indifference, or letting go, which is similar to a pattern I developed in waterskiing. To improve my skill, I had to be willing to let go and risk falling as I made a turn, knowing that after the turn, I usually would regain my control. In a session, when I let go of my agenda for change and am fully present with the client, I can focus completely on what he is experiencing in the moment, such as when he says, "This is why I couldn't follow through with our goals last week." At this moment in the session, I might say something like, "Yes, I can see why you didn't," or "I can see how hard that must be." I surrender to the turn. Anytime I feel myself wanting to yes–but or argue with the client, I try to remember the energy of letting go in waterskiing. I might follow up the empathy with a question such as, "What might work better?" rather than try to problem-solve on my own. If waterskiing is not your thing, draw on a significant experience in your own history as a metaphor for knowing when to let go in the therapy session.

Be Fascinated by and Accepting of Ambivalence

Rather than focus on outcomes, we need to become fascinated by the process of dealing with pathological ambivalence. There is a wealth of information embedded in the two sides of any dilemma. Be curious about the reasons for the ambivalence and the wisdom and fear on both sides. It is easy to react to one side of the ambivalence as healthy and the other as unhealthy. For instance, in recovery from an eating disorder, nearly every patient has a part of herself that wants to recover and a part that doesn't want to recover. On the surface, of course, we would assume that the part that doesn't want to recover is wrong, unhealthy, or, at best, misguided. However, when listening closely to the reasons, we learn so much more about the patient and her inner life.

One patient, Amber, realized that she was afraid to give up her symptom of purging because it provided her with a sense, albeit false, that she could make up for mistakes and "wipe the slate clean." This feeling seemed extremely necessary for her to experience daily. As we explored this need, she began to identify a narrative that she told herself, somewhat subconsciously, that she was unclean and thus had to do something to make herself believe, even if just for a few minutes, that she was clean. The purge had become a symbolic attempt to help her get something that she desperately felt she needed. She needed to find a way to believe that she was good, but she had only been able to come up with a temporary fix.

The harder Amber and I worked on strategies to delay or prevent the purging, the more we were missing the primary problem. She was initially confused and ashamed that she couldn't use skills that she was given to decrease this "bad" behavior, which conversely increased her need to rid herself of perceived shame through purging. Becoming fascinated with her ambivalence opened us up to helping her find other ways to feel pure and to explore the original reasons for her sense of shame.

It is also very empowering when a patient senses that you are accepting of her ambivalence. Lakeesha was being treated for an eating disorder in a partial hospital program. She was 17 and had been encouraged to attend by her parents but was resistant to the process, which would require that she gain weight to go to college the following fall. Lakeesha would generally look bored and distracted when in groups. Her affect was fairly flat, although she did occasionally reveal a dry sense of humor in her complaints about the program. In a dialectical behavioral therapy group that I was leading, I asked her if she was intending to come across as bored and she said, "So, what? Am I supposed to pretend to be interested even if I'm not?' I was somewhat taken aback, but part of me was very impressed by the strength and spunk she displayed toward an adult in what could be perceived as an authority position. Of course, the rest of the group members held their breath to see how I'd respond. After a short pause, I grinned and said, "Yes! That's just what we're going for here, you are so insightful!" To which she smiled in spite of herself, and the group collectively sighed with relief. Later in a meal group, someone was talking about a movie star with a dry wit. I leaned over to Lakeesha and whispered (in a voice that everyone could hear) "You probably wouldn't relate." She said, "No, not at all." We developed a strong and playful relationship. One day, I attempted a similar strategy, and it didn't produce the grin that it usually did. I said, "Lakeesha, you don't feel like playing today?" To which she responded with a sad face, "No, I'm too upset today." She then began to talk openly.

I think that pointing out Lakeesha's behavior in a playful manner communicated a sense of acceptance while still making my point. Being a rule follower as a child, I am able to admire people who hold their ground even if it's not in their best interest. I think they sense this acceptance, which enables them to trust and risk change. I encourage you to be fascinated with your ambivalent clients and respect any strengths that you see.

Remember That Ambivalence Is Intrapsychic

If your patient is not following your recommendations, there is good reason. This doesn't mean, however, that you aren't making good recommendations. It may simply mean that the patient must get off the "ambivalence fence" before he can follow them. The patient is in pain, torn up inside. Thus, what looks like resistance to you or resistance to change is internal to the patient. Realize that the client needs to repeat the painful past while also wishing for things to change. It is like being at an internal crossroads and not knowing which path to choose. This indecision can seem paralyzing to the patient.

Develop Skills That Empower the Patient to Take Responsibility for Change

The dialectical concept of responsibility for change as 100% on the therapist and 100% on the client means that the therapist is extremely active and directive in facilitating the client to take full responsibility for her change. It might seem to make more sense to say the responsibility is 50–50. But my experience is that we are both doing 100% of the work. I'm not working at only half-mast, and neither is the client. We are working on different tasks that are closely linked and interdependent.

The patient needs to feel that most of the change can be credited to his courage and hard work rather than to your brilliance as a therapist. Sometimes, even playing confused can be a very powerful intervention. A great example is the character Columbo, played by Peter Falk in the 1970s TV detective series of the same name. He often knew exactly who the murderer was but would play dumb, tricking the culprit into talking more and thus revealing him or her as the guilty party. Columbo's technique was effective because he appeared so unthreatening: He wore a trademark rumpled khaki raincoat to complement unruly hair and a (real-life) glass eye, making his way around crime scenes with a crooked posture and pained, shuffling gait. His manner was of a doddering, befuddled uncle. Characters couldn't help but open up; he seemed so clueless. And then, wham! He nailed 'em.

I became fascinated with Columbo's style and began incorporating it into my work with ambivalent patients in the early 1990s—not because I wanted to play dumb, but because I realized that although I understood the person was ambivalent, I often didn't really appreciate the wisdom on both sides. This wisdom was what the client had to reveal. Although we aren't trying to trick our clients into confessions, I do think there are many things we can learn from Columbo's style of questioning. If we look like we are curious but don't have all the answers, we are better able to elicit clients' ability to investigate for themselves by looking inward at their own motivations. We may know where we want our clients to go, but we lead through facilitation of their own curiosity to find their own answers.

For example, I was working with a teenaged male who came in each week, sat down, and gave me one-word answers to my questions. He gradually would talk more as the session went on. I knew that he was hesitant to trust me and uncomfortable talking about his feelings, so I kept asking questions until he opened up. I also knew that he perceived his mother as very critical and believed that she didn't listen to or understand him. After about the third session, I was ready to point out the pattern. I had chosen to spend the first few sessions convincing him through my questions that this was a safe place to explore feelings. Then I knew it was time to move forward.

I thought about reflecting these observations to him and interpreting his behavior. It would have sounded something like this: "Jake, I've noticed that you come in to our sessions acting like you don't want to be here, giving me abrupt, one-word answers to my questions. But then you become more talkative as the session continues. I'm wondering if you are hesitant at first to open up because you fear that I'm going to judge you or, in some way, react the way your mother does." Not a bad interpretation. However, this kind of reflection could lead to pitfalls. If he acknowledged some truth to my comment, I would then be tempted to try and reassure him that I was not going to behave like his mother. In other words, I would be engaging in a split—me against his mother.

Instead, I decided not to interpret. I mentioned that I was confused as to why in our sessions he started out looking down and giving abrupt answers as if he resented my questions, but then opened up later in the session. I then stopped talking and waited for him to respond. He paused to consider this for several moments. I sensed that it was the first time he had given it much thought. In this moment, I had been 100% responsible in asking the particular question that enabled him to take 100% responsibility in searching for his truth and deciding how to proceed. He then went into much detail about how it felt for him to walk in each week. Had I simply commented to him that it might be because he was uncomfortable talking about his feelings, he wouldn't have had the benefit of exploring his own motivations and doing the internal work to come up with the same interpretation for himself. Moreover, my interpretations, even when correct, probably wouldn't completely capture the richness of his experience. In Jake's case, I believe that most, if not all, of the progress in that session happened during that pause.

Develop Strong Interpersonal Boundaries

It is important for therapists to get our own interpersonal needs met outside of the work setting. This doesn't mean that we don't experience great fulfillment by our work, but that we have most of our basic needs met elsewhere. For instance, when I am feeling less secure in life, I have a stronger need to be seen as helpful at work, making me more likely to want to make brilliant interpretations or be seen as extremely caring. Similarly, it is important to remember that you are who you are, with worth and unique strengths and weaknesses regardless of how your client is doing or feeling toward you in the moment.

Monitor and Use Your Reactions to the Client

If a therapist is feeling bored, it might be that the client is spending too much time talking *about* things rather than working on change. As I mentioned earlier, I think that some of the most powerful moments of a therapy session occur when the client is pausing to ponder something new. After a well-placed question, if the client pauses, I attribute that to having new thoughts.

If the therapist finds herself dreading the session with a particular client, this is also valuable information. In my experience, this usually occurs when a client is not changing or growing, and the relationship is stuck in certain patterns. This is the time to start exploring ambivalence.

Monitor How the Client Is Reacting to You

It also is important to be aware of how the client is reacting to you. Another dialectic in therapy often involves the client asking for help and then feeling threatened by that help. The client might see you as someone trying to take something vitally important from him, or he might put you on a pedestal as a savior-like figure, as when a patient tells you that "You're the best therapist I've ever had!"

Assessment

Assessment in the context of this book focuses directly on factors related to pathological ambivalence. Other types of assessment may have occurred in the course of psychotherapy, but as pathological ambivalence surfaces, it becomes important to assess beliefs, problematic behaviors that arise from the beliefs, the function of symptoms, and the motivation for change. This form of assessment may occur at any time during psychotherapy.

Assessing Previously Formed Beliefs

The first focus of therapy when addressing pathological ambivalence is to identify conscious and unconscious beliefs. I recommend doing a structured and thorough assessment of beliefs that inform the person's life so that the therapist won't be surprised when they appear in the therapeutic process. These beliefs weave together to form narratives that were presumably functional at one point but now are interfering with the client's ability to have a satisfying life. I use a worksheet to assess beliefs about self, others, emotions, and the world (see Appendix A). Many people will project their old scripts on any event regardless of how distorted the projection is. This is why a thorough assessment of beliefs from childhood is so important. When a patient is experiencing pathological ambivalence, corrective experiences aren't sufficient unless there is mindful attention to the beliefs which need to shift. Generally speaking, it isn't every hurtful experience that must be "healed" but that the common beliefs formed in the context of these experiences need to be shifted.

Assessing Dysfunctional Behaviors Motivated by Belief

The next step is to address the ways in which the client's beliefs affect the behaviors that need to be decreased. Not only do the beliefs affect behavior, the behavior then functions to reinforce the belief. For example, if a person believes that the world is dangerous, it is likely that he will reduce his behavioral repertoire by avoiding interactions he may perceive as dangerous. This avoidance, in turn, prevents him from learning that sometimes the world is not dangerous. The client can be asked to fill in the blanks of the following sentence to help him understand some of the reasons for her ambivalence and therefore why it is hard to change.

> I have a need for _____, which I use [my symptom] to meet because I have not yet been able to believe_____. I continue this way even though it makes me_____.

This could be completed to read:

> "I have a need for acceptance for which I use perfectionism and overachieving because I can't yet believe that I am important. This persists even though I am exhausted."

The client can then see that continuing to attempt to be accepted through perfectionism is doomed to failure, because even if she does receive acceptance, she is likely to credit the acceptance to her overachievement rather than to the person she is on a more authentic level. This simply reinforces the original and exhausting belief. See Appendix A for a sample worksheet that I use to help clients to see the trap and self-fulfilling prophecy embedded in their narratives and then to generate alternative actions.

As clients complete these worksheets, they begin to clarify the narratives they've created, and the therapist can learn a lot about the client in a short amount of time without having to do much interpretation or confrontation. As these beliefs begin to present themselves in the therapeutic process, the clinician can gently ask if the current feeling or behavior might be related to the belief the client had identified earlier. Using the clients' own words is so much more powerful than "calling them out."

Assessing the Function of the Symptom

It is helpful not only to assess how beliefs affect behavior, but also to work from the other direction by assessing how the symptom is functioning to satisfy a need. Clients often benefit from understanding how a problematic behavior is functioning for them to facilitate developing new ways to function.

For clients suffering with pathological ambivalence, the symptoms are functioning, dialectically, to get a core need met without having to risk the fear and expectation that the essential need will not be met. As described in John's story (see Chapter 2), his symptom was to take care of others without becoming vulnerable. This caretaking served to give him some of the pseudo-experience of being loved without having to become entirely vulnerable, because he believed that the person eventually would leave.

It is ineffective and generally premature for a therapist to attempt to take away something that a client is holding on to until you both understand why it's being held and recognize that the client will need something else to hold on to in its place. The scariest moment in any self-improvement endeavor occurs just as an old behavior is being relinquished. At that moment, it can feel as if the client is freefalling. We therapists need to be very sensitive to this experience. Terry explained it to me this way: "It feels like I am standing with my back to a cliff and you are suggesting that I take a step backward." After thoroughly empathizing with how awful that must feel, I asked him to consider the possibility that since he's facing backward, he might not realize that it's only a small drop. If he can turn and look at it with me (by exploring the function of the symptom), he may see that he can actually take that step.

Nina seemed to be plagued with crises. Every week she faced a new catastrophe in her life. It seemed that each session was just putting out the current fire while nothing was happening to help her make changes that would last. We both were caught up in the feeling that life was just very unfair to her and she couldn't catch a break. Eventually, though, it emerged that she was creating much of the chaos through choices that she made. Initially, I was very tempted to point this out to her; however, the crises felt so painful and real that I knew my interpreting it as a pattern would be too invalidating and might lead to shame. Instead, I shifted to assessment.

First, after assessing her core beliefs, she recognized that as a child whose parents were divorced and whose mother struggled with depression, she had begun to believe that she wasn't important. Second, we used the functions checklist, and she identified that having crises and chaos in her life was a way for her to get attention from others and therefore gain a short-term sense of importance. Finally, I did an assessment of her earliest recollections, one of which related to breaking her leg and getting help and attention from her mother while she was in a cast. Nina had grown up feeling as if people would only notice her if she were in crisis. As a result of these assessments, Nina recognized that she made sense. She was able to see that any child with these circumstances and a little resourcefulness might learn to use crises to get needs met. Incidentally, if I had simply interpreted this for her, it may have sounded very foreign and judgmental. Imagine telling her that she was creating crises to get attention. Some of these incidents had to do with being mistreated, and I would have appeared to be blaming the victim, which might have resulted in her feeling guilt or shame, as well as being angry with me.

For Nina, being in crisis was related to her core need for love and worth. Conversely, she came to understand that the crises also functioned to protect and distance her in relationships. This was related to a need for safety. Nina assumed that people would not think she was worth their love and that eventually they would reject her. She tended to burn out her relationships and usually ended up lonely. It became clear that this behavior was perfectly matched to her conflicting needs. It made sense to her that she would use crises as a focal point in relationships—and in therapy sessions—given her beliefs and early experiences. She also concluded that if she didn't address her needs in a new way her behaviors could keep her stuck forever courting chaos.

By using an assessment to determine the function of her symptom, Nina explored this without feeling judged or blamed by me. This allowed her to explore the part of her that would want to keep the behavior, which greatly reduced resistance and became the catalyst for change.

Symptoms often function to distract from painful emotions, relieve stress, increase a sense of control, and provide comfort. A generically generated list can help a client brainstorm on possible functions of his symptoms. The following are common functions based on core needs which can be used by asking the client to check off any phrase which seems to strike them as a possibility. A more exhaustive list is found in Linehan's workbook (1993).

_____ Gives you a feeling of control

_____ Provides a temporary sense of purpose and a break from boredom

_____ Distracts from painful emotions

_____ Serves as a pretext for avoiding daily activities

_____ Gives you a logical escape from responsibilities

_____ Justifies time for yourself

_____ Alleviates stress

_____ Provides comfort

_____ Serves as an explanation for failure or fear of failure

_____ Provides a sense of identity

_____ Draws other people's attention

_____ Gives a sense of stimulation or excitement

_____ Reduces anxiety

_____ Justifies difficulty with addressing ambivalent feelings with making decisions

_____ Helps you avoid getting too close in relationships

Assessing the Level of Motivation

A person caught in pathological ambivalence often appears as if she is not motivated to change. The truth is, only one part of her is afraid to change; there is also a part that wants to change, or the client wouldn't be in therapy. Even in cases where the person is court-ordered or brought by her parents (discussed in Chapter 6), there is usually a part of her that wants things to be different in her life. As noted throughout this book, it is important to assess the motivation of *both* parts of the dilemma. Motivational interviewing offers many strategies for dealing with assessing motivation (Sobel & Sobel, 2008). Many of these strategies are helpful in assessing the motivation of both parts, such as asking questions that evoke change talk as well as asking open-ended questions about reasons for not wanting to change or to wait or to go slow. People who work with pathologically ambivalent individuals will find the strategies of motivational interviewing invaluable in helping clients harness and move through the stuck points.

Erin was struggling with ambivalence related to changing her job. She was not very happy in her career but could not motivate herself to start looking at other possibilities. She worked as an accountant, and although she was very good at her job, she was dissatisfied and bored. She was beginning to get depressed and had been prescribed an antidepressant. She was artistic, but because she had excelled in math, her father and instructors had encouraged her to go into accounting. She assumed that it was right for her because she did so well in this area.

When asked open-ended questions about her thoughts about quitting her job, she described that she didn't feel happy and dreaded going to work every day. She was afraid that if she didn't quit, she might get so depressed that she would become suicidal. At this point, her therapist was strongly tempted to advise her to quit her job because it seemed as if her very life could be at stake.

However, when Erin was asked open-ended questions about why she stayed with her job, such as, "What keeps you from making the decision to quit?" she was just as persuasive about how important it was for her to do something worthwhile. She explained that she knew she was helping others and that being an artist seemed like such a self-focused endeavor. Additionally, she enjoyed the lifestyle that she was able to afford and knew that she couldn't continue it as an artist. Finally, she enjoyed the relationship she had with her dad in talking about business and knew that he would never be able to relate to her love of art. On a deeper level, she also identified a belief that "my needs are not as important as others."

Erin was ping-ponging between polarities, making it impossible to come to a decision. Through motivational interviewing, she began to recognize that there was value in both paths and that neither was right or wrong. By doing an *assessment of beliefs*, she noticed that she held an automatic belief from childhood that needed to be reevaluated. She recognized that she was not trapped and that she needed to find a path that honored as many of her values as possible. Through *values clarification*, she recognized that lifestyle was less important, but her relationship with her dad was extremely important. Erin decided to have an honest talk with him to help her make a decision. Over time, she took small steps toward a decision, which incorporated values from both sides of the dilemma. She ended up shifting to contract work as an accountant, which enabled her to take art classes.

An eager therapist might have been be tempted to steer Erin toward making a choice to alleviate her depression. However, her current job may not have been the source of her distress. Instead, it was her inability to find the value in both sides of her dilemma. Had she made a choice either way without first honoring her ambivalence, she would have lost things that were of significant value to her. This approach was much more effective, in part because it is impossible for a therapist to be fully aware of all the values that are at play in any given dilemma.

After a thorough assessment of beliefs, dysfunctional behaviors, functions of symptoms and motivation has been conducted, treatment planning can ensue. It is important to develop specific behavioral goals that are mutually agreed on between the therapist and client. See

Appendix B for suggestions for behaviorally oriented treatment planning specifically toward dealing with pathological ambivalence.

Increasing Awareness of Ambivalence Through Psychoeducation

Being as transparent as possible about your impressions, goals, and choice of strategies in psychotherapy enables a more collaborative atmosphere. Education may involve statements such as, "A lot of people in this situation think ... Do you relate to that?" or "Let me tell you what I think might be happening." It is important to distinguish between educating about things that are generally true of human nature, development, emotions, and brain functioning as qualitatively different from giving advice, making interpretations, or falling into splits. Generally, I follow the education with "How does that fit for you?" or "What does your mind do with that information?" so that you are still encouraging the clients' curiosity and self-awareness. Later in this chapter, I describe the areas of psychoeducation that are most pertinent to dealing with pathological ambivalence.

When people are struggling with pathological ambivalence, it is helpful to use a common language in discussions of issues contributing to ambivalence. By educating the client about your philosophy as it relates to problem development and change, you develop a more collaborative relationship. The following topics are essential to address when dealing with pathological ambivalence as they are related to the nature of ambivalence and the factors which increase the vulnerability to developing pathological ambivalence.

The Nature of Ambivalence or Resistance to Change

When educating clients about ambivalence, I like to use the image of a triangle. Here is a simple example: Joanie has been asked by friends to go to dinner and a movie, but she needs to study for an exam.

Go to dinner only (2 hours)

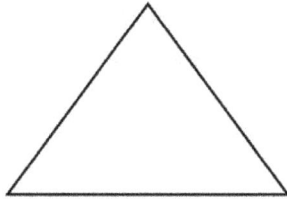

Stay home & study (4 hrs)   OR   Go to dinner & movie (4 hrs)

The two points at the bottom of the triangle represent the two sides of the dilemma. As long as the person is focusing only on these two points, she may be stuck because neither side provides her with a solution. There is *value* for her in either decision. She is torn because her grades are important to her, but building relationships is also very important. Either choice can cause her to neglect one of her values. For instance, if she focuses on staying home, she loses the positive aspects of going out with her friends, and if she goes out, she will not get the grade that she wants on her project. To complicate the matter, Joanie may be more consciously aware of one value over the other. She may think that she *should* value school work more than going out. In this way, she may be failing to recognize building friendships as a real value. She is likely to be telling herself that she *should* stay home.

Resolving this dilemma will require her to look more closely at the pros and cons to *each* side rather than simply moving between the two points on the base of the triangle. She may need to clarify for herself what values are involved on both sides so that she's not governed by a rule that she has established for herself. As she explores her ambivalence in this way, she is more likely to see room for compromise. As she dismisses the negative aspects of the dilemma and focuses on the positives of each side, her brain may spontaneously create a solution that can honor the positives, such as going only to dinner.

Through a cost–benefit or pros-and-cons analysis, the triangles might not always be equilateral: If there are more reasons to stay home and study, for example, then the resolution may be skewed in one direction. Another option could be to study for 3 hours and meet for appetizers for 1. You may already be saying, "But what if there are three or more options?" In that case, the triangle would look three-dimensional, with all base points connecting to the same tip. Four options would look like a square on the bottom, and so forth. The more options along the base, the more the image will begin to look like a cone. Life can be that complicated at times, but the same principles apply. Each base point needs to be explored with a goal of capturing the positive elements while letting go of the negative ones. This will allow movement up toward the top point.

Sensitive Personality

As was explained in Chapter 2, a large percentage of the people who come to therapy may be characterized as highly sensitive. About 20% of the population is highly sensitive, according to research (Acevedo et al., 2014), which also is uncovering evidence that physiological sensitivity is related, at least in part, to the neurotransmitter serotonin. I thoroughly review this with most of my patients and often encourage them to buy one the many books on this subject (Aron, 1996; Zeff, 2004) .

Pathological Ambivalence and Self-Abandonment

When a person has pathological ambivalence, she may experience something akin to grief as she tries to choose a side, since both sides have some wisdom. I explain to my patients that they have been stuck because it feels as if they are abandoning a part of themselves if they try to choose as side. For example, Jessie wanted help for panic attacks and was afraid to drive for fear that a panic attack would occur. Jessie also was an extreme perfectionist. As her therapy progressed, she began to see that her panic attacks were related to thoughts of a perfectionistic nature. If she couldn't do something perfectly, she became paralyzed and did nothing at all. When she berated herself for doing nothing, the panic increased.

The more I tried to help her reevaluate her perfectionism, the more anxious and depressed Jessie became. We had to slow down and work on understanding why the perfectionism was so important. When Jessie tried to act with less perfectionism—for example, by admitting to a mistake—the part that feared rejection felt abandoned. However, when she attempted to be perfect, another part of her felt abandoned, unlovable, and burdened. Jessie needed to connect to both parts of herself rather than just try to block the perfectionism. She began to realize that the perfectionism had served a purpose and maybe even helped her in childhood but was no longer useful. Therefore, she was able to understand that, although giving it up might cause fear and depression, it was still necessary to achieving her therapeutic goals. She needed to encourage the part of her that clung to the perfectionism by finding other ways to feel power and worth.

Symptom Development and Function

Jessie's crippling perfectionism made sense in light of her story. I believe that most people's thoughts, feelings, habits, and behaviors make sense, no matter how dysfunctional they seem in the moment. At Atlanta Center for Eating Disorders we use the concept of *respecting the symptom*— quite a feat when you consider that eating disorders result in more fatalities than all other mental disorders (Arcelus, Mitchell, Wales, & Nielsen, 2011; Smink, Van Hoeke, & Hoek, 2012). Respecting the symptom means studying the symptom and the surrounding urges, thoughts, and feelings in an effort to learn from them. We educate our clients to turn their mind *toward* this endeavor rather than trying to avoid it because we know that unless we understand the ways in which the symptom behaviors are actually helping, the client won't be able to give them up.

Often the symptom is used as a temporary way of managing ambivalence. When a person is experiencing an unmet need but doesn't believe he is worthy of having the need met, the symptom can act as both a substitute for the need as well as a distraction from feeling the pain of the unmet need. It allows the person to proceed in life without having to face the extreme anxiety of risking an attempt to get the need met or the extreme shame of going without. Thus, the symptom can tell us where the "ouch" is.

Window of Opportunity Journaling is a strategy I employ to help clients understand the function of their symptoms. The best time to identify the reason for an urge that results in problematic behaviors is in the moment when the feelings are intense. Possibly everything one needs to know about why he is struggling is captured in the feelings at those moments. I call this a window of opportunity. If a client waits until later (for example, describing the event at a therapy session the next day), it is much more difficult to capture the urges and impulses that she had at the time she engaged in the symptom behavior.

I suggest to clients that when they feel these intense urges, they pause and take a few minutes to write down some of what they are feeling in the moment, and then bring it into their next session to talk over with the therapist.

To facilitate the experience of pausing during this window of opportunity I give my clients a handout (see Appendix A) with the following questions, explaining that the questions are just a starting point and that they can write about anything that comes to mind. I also suggest writing for 15 minutes (some set a timer). After that, if they still want to engage in the symptom or behavior (with the exception of behaviors that hurt others or are suicidal or self-harming in nature), they can go ahead and do so, but should still consider the endeavor a success, as they have taken an important step in increasing their self-awareness.

> What am I feeling right now (in "feeling" words such as anger, hurt, etc.)?
> What changes am I aware of in my body as I'm feeling this emotion (stomach, jaw shoulders, etc.)?
> What happened to make me feel this way?
> Is this a familiar feeling in that it comes up often?
> Could this feeling be related to ways I felt as a child, and, if so, how?
> When was the first time I ever felt this way, and what was happening then?
> What did I need then but didn't get?
> How would engaging in _____ help with this feeling?
> How would I feel immediately after engaging in _____?
> How would I feel later?
> What would happen if I didn't engage in _____?
> When someone is feeling this way, what do they truly need?
> What do I need from myself when I am feeling this way?
> Is there anything I can do other than engaging in _____ that would help even a little?

I've found that when people work on this for 15 minutes, at the critical moment, something important almost always happens. However, many can't begin at this level. In these situations, I suggest starting with whatever they *can* do. For instance, the first step may simply be buying the journal and placing it in a strategic location. Next, they might only have the ability to open it and write one word, preferably a feeling word. A creative variation on this is to have a box of crayons near the journal, and they can choose a color to match the emotion. Next time, they might write just one phrase, then a sentence, and then write for 5 minutes and so on. It is important that small successes are celebrated. Additionally, some people are very averse to writing, so we might explore other avenues such as dictating into a phone, for example. People may not want to write because it seems tedious. Although any starting point is a good one, I generally tell people that there is something very powerful about handwriting in that it slows the brain and can function as a communication to themselves that they are worth the time and effort. Finally, with clients who simply can't yet pause in the moment, I will suggest that as soon as possible after engaging in the behavior, they use the handout.

Perfectionism

As in the earlier example of Jessie, for people who are motivated by perfectionism, it can be very difficult to even consider compromise. These individuals often get bogged down attempting to find the perfect solution. They have the false belief that if there is a right or wrong in every matter. They are often motivated by avoidance, making decisions based more on avoiding disappointing others or disappointing themselves than on wisdom. Perfectionism is different from working hard: The difference between these concepts lies in the motivation. Working hard to achieve a goal is fundamentally different from working hard to avoid something. What look like similar problem-solving strategies on the surface often carry varying emotional valences. Educating clients about their perfectionism often is the first step to moving through ambivalence.

Factors Involved in Producing Emotion

Attempting to explore pathological ambivalence can lead to intense emotional reactions. To be able to regulate our emotions, it helps if we are fully aware of the many factors that can create an emotional reaction. Everyone understands that emotions are generally related to an event.

But it can be so much more complicated than that. The following are topics that I go over with patients so that they can become their own "experts" in the area of emotions.

Events and Their Interpretation. When most of us consider what has caused an emotional response, we generally think of some kind of an event, for example, feeling happy at my birthday party or hurt by something someone said. However, an emotional experience is a very complicated occurrence of which the event is only one of many factors. The way the event is interpreted is also key to understanding the emotions produced. Consider this illustration:

Mary and Dana are riding the elevator at work. Joy, whom they both know, enters the elevator without speaking to them. Dana reacts by retracing in her mind recent conversations she's had with Joy to figure out what she's done wrong to offend her. In contrast, Mary begins to wonder if Joy is feeling okay. As they head to their offices, Dana avoids Joy, going straight to her desk. She is thinking about a conversation she had with Joy a while back in which they had what she interpreted as a friendly difference of opinion. She begins to feel irritated with Joy for holding a grudge over something so minor. It makes her feel the way she did as a child when she felt like she could never express her own opinion without someone getting mad.

Meanwhile, Mary approaches Joy and asks if everything is okay. Joy explains that she was lost in thought about an upsetting phone call she just got from her son's teacher and apologizes for not speaking. Mary offers support and their relationship strengthens, while Dana continues to avoid Joy, who is oblivious to the reason and never understands why their relationship seemed to have cooled.

We've all probably been in Mary or Dana's position at some point. When our reaction to an event triggers old feelings, we tend to interpret the event in light of the past situation and project our interpretation instead of examining the facts of the current moment. Our clients need to be aware of this process when it occurs and to be taught how to consider the present as is. They need to become aware of their "trigger points" and habitual ways of interpreting events, based on narratives from the past, which may be operating unconsciously. Dana is feeling pain that occurred a long time ago and missing opportunities in her current life situation that could be healing.

Brain Functioning. It is also helpful to provide education about brain functioning, cognitive development and connectivity as has already been described earlier in this book. I developed the term *idling emotion* to describe the phenomenon of emotional habits. The idling emotion is the *most often experienced negative childhood emotion*. This is where we *idle* out of habit. Notice the emphasis on the word negative. Due to the increased imprinting when we are scared or mad, negative emotions have a more immediate and lasting effect on the brain than positive emotions. I tell my patients that I used to feel guilty about being a "glass-half-empty" person because there was so much for which I should feel grateful. However, the more I've learned about brain functioning, the more I've come to believe that it is natural to be a glass half-empty person. As discussed in greater detail in Chapter 1, there is more survival value in knowing where the bear lives than where the daffodils grow. The good news, however, is that through mindful awareness, we can train our brains to focus more on the positive. Consequently, even if a person has had a good childhood, it is possible that he still has a negative idling emotion. It is helpful to identify that habitual emotion, so that we know when it is operating. Otherwise, we are at risk for perpetuating the emotion by seeking circumstances to match it. I often advise patients, as a homework assignment, to consider during the week what their idling emotion is. No one has yet told me that she didn't think she had an idling emotion.

I also teach my clients that brain functioning affects assumptions that people make in childhood, which in turn leads to narratives that can cause negative emotions. It is helpful for them to understand that young children make assumptions based on association rather than causation. Therefore, when bad things happen, children often believe that they are not good enough or are unlovable. As they head into adolescence, they begin to be able to think abstractly and can begin forming rules in their mind about how to best operate in their environment. These rules are based on their earlier beliefs. As adolescents, they may begin telling themselves statements such as, "In order to make Dad happy, I must be perfect," or "People will think I'm silly, so I should be quiet."

Putting away childish things means rethinking these automatic beliefs. They are difficult to change, as they have made very strong neural pathways in our brains relating to the number of times they've been repeated in our thoughts. I explain to my patients that this is why it is okay to offer themselves affirmations such as "I am worthy and lovable," even if they don't believe them yet because they are building neuronal pathways.

Chemical Factors. Some clients may not be aware of the interaction between chemical factors and mood. For example, if a person is feeling sluggish, he might interpret this as sadness—and one can always find something to feel sad about.

I educate my clients that emotions are accompanied by physical and chemical reactions in the body. The clearest example of this is that if you get sad enough, a drop of water falls out of your eye. Kind of strange when you think of it, isn't it? When an emotion is experienced, the limbic system produces chemicals. If you remember something sad, your brain produces different chemicals than if you remember something happy. Until the chemicals dissipate, you will tend see things through the *lens* of chemicals currently in your body. So, if you get mad, even though you talk about it and take care of the situation, the chemicals may linger. Because your brain is always looking for homeostasis, you are more likely to focus on things that make you mad, prolonging the chemical event of anger (ever awakened on the wrong side of the bed and felt that way all day?).

I refer to this as the *burnt food syndrome*. When I've burned food, there is a pungent odor that permeates my entire house. Even after I've thoroughly cleaned the pan, the aroma lingers. However, this doesn't mean that I need to clean another pan. It might help, however, to spray air freshener. Similarly, when we get mad or hurt, the chemicals linger, and if we are mindful of this, we have the power to shift the chemicals in our brain on purpose. For instance, you could call someone who makes you laugh. Then your brain will produce happy chemicals.

Chemicals that we ingest can also greatly affect our mood. Consider a person who gets up in the morning and has coffee (a stimulant), later in the day has a glass of wine (a depressant) and smokes a cigarette (a stimulant), maybe takes a cold pill (a stimulant), and then before bed takes an antidepressant and Nyquil to sleep. Each of these can affect one's mood in a different way.

Hunger also produces chemicals that can affect emotion. When the body has not taken in enough calories for the effort expended, it will produce adrenalin as a false fuel, so to speak, to enable the person to search for food. This results in what many have experienced as "the shakes" when they've skipped a meal. It is very useful to produce adrenalin if, for example, you are living in the wild and there is a snowstorm. The adrenalin motivates you to keep going until a food source can be located. However, if you are simply sitting at your desk and have forgotten to stop for lunch, this adrenalin can be misinterpreted as anxiety. It is the same chemical produced as when we are scared or threatened. If we don't label it as a result of hunger, we could mistakenly attribute the increased agitation to emotions or thoughts. Because in our busy lives we can always find something to be anxious about, we may misinterpret the experience as worry, or we may overreact to situations or thoughts which are worrisome.

Fatigue and poor sleep can increase susceptibility to the experience of negative emotions. A common acronym in Alcoholics Anonymous is HALT: hungry, angry, lonely, tired. Recovering addicts are urged to HALT—that is, to stop when experiencing any of these conditions—because they are at increased risk of using substances. In general, fatigue and poor sleep make us more vulnerable to any negative emotions that we may experience (Krystal, 2006; Linehan, 1993).

Finally, some people seem to be quite affected by weather such as the well-researched phenomenon called SAD, seasonal affective disorder. Experts aren't sure what causes SAD. But they think it may be caused by a lack of sunlight. Lack of light may upset your "biological clock," which controls your sleep–wake pattern and other circadian rhythms. Another explanation is that it might cause problems with serotonin, a brain chemical that affects mood. Other people are affected by barometric changes.

Personality Disorders

Because some people who struggle with pathological ambivalence may be diagnosed with personality disorders, therapists need to be comfortable educating these individuals about the meaning of the diagnosis. As has been discussed, pathological ambivalence has features in common with borderline personality disorder. When working with someone who meets the criteria for a personality disorder, I try to approach it in a manner that normalizes it as much as possible while providing hope. It is helpful to approach it from both a nature and a nurture perspective. When it is clear that the person has suffered abuse or neglect in childhood, I refer back to the Victor Frankl (1946) quote, "an abnormal reaction to an abnormal situation is normal" (p. 32). If traumatic things were occurring when the person's personality was forming, then, of course, they could develop a personality disorder. That would be normal.

Many people who have been given this diagnosis have assumed that their condition is very difficult to overcome, as was assumed by experts for many years. I educate these people about recent research related to increased susceptibility to stress such as in the area of serotonin, as reviewed in Chapter 2. I reassure them that they can learn skills to manage their sensitivity by improving their ability to reevaluate the scripts which they formed in childhood about the world and themselves. In this way, we demystify the label of borderline personality disorder and proceed with treatment in the same way that I would with anyone with ambivalence.

The Shame–Regret Continuum

One area of great confusion for people with pathological ambivalence is in feelings related to shame, guilt, and regret. Although people may use these words slightly differently from how they are presented here, it can be helpful to tease apart these related experiences in a practical, concrete way. The types of experience are differentiated based on the thoughts associated with the feeling, the types of events that elicit the feeling, the typical duration and the associated action urge. The therapeutic goal is to move from shame to regret.

Toxic shame is qualitatively different from all other emotions because unlike most emotions, which motivate us to do something protective (e.g., anger prompts us to protect ourselves), shame tends to inhibit motion. Toxic shame doesn't motivate action to protect the individual; instead, it affects identity. The thoughts that accompany toxic shame are identity thoughts, such as "I am bad." It is my experience that shame often occurs when an individual accepts responsibility for another person's wrongdoing, such as "If I were lovable, he wouldn't hit me; therefore, I am not lovable." People are especially vulnerable to developing toxic shame in early childhood before the development of abstract thought and myelination of the prefrontal lobes. A review of Piaget's cognitive development in Chapter 2 elaborates on this point. Extremely sensitive individuals are also more vulnerable to developing toxic shame even in normal conditions. Additionally, toxic shame can motivate perfectionism as a way of attempting to find worth when feeling unlovable, inadequate or bad.

John Bradshaw (1988) writes about the concept of healthy shame. I find it difficult to conceptualize the two words of healthy and shame together in one concept, but he describes a helpful distinction between toxic shame and healthy shame. After bringing up this dilemma with patients, we came up with the term *natural humility* to describe the same phenomenon. Thus, natural humility is the momentary feeling of embarrassment over doing something wrong or silly, for example, that any human might do at one point or another, such as tripping and falling. An initial reaction might be embarrassment, but it is short-lived, and we can usually laugh it off. Toxic shame, however, can last a lifetime.

Guilt is an appropriate emotion in response to doing something wrong. Guilt motivates a corrective behavior, such as learning from our mistake or apologizing for the wrongdoing. The experience of guilt is difficult to set aside until a corrective action is taken but then should dissipate quickly—unlike toxic shame, which persists because there is no action that can be taken that eradicates it. The thoughts that accompany guilt are focused on an action versus the identity statements of toxic shame: "I did wrong" versus "I am bad." Many people use the words *guilt* and *shame* synonymously. But they are very different, and clients will benefit from seeing how they differ so that they can move through them.

Regret: I think of regret as "guilt light." Regret is an emotion that people feel when they've acted in a way that isn't in line with their values but they've done all they can to correct the situation. The person has learned from the mistake and made whatever reparations possible. Unlike the experience of guilt, with regret, there is nothing more that can be done. Regret may linger because the memory of the wrongdoing is still present, and the person may always feel something when thinking about it. Regret is a gentle reminder of a person's values. Although it may continue long term, regret only arises when something prompts the memory and one can easily shift to other feelings. There is no action urge embedded in the experience of regret.

Many clients who struggle with pathological ambivalence do not know how to differentiate among these various experiences. See Appendix C for a worksheet titled "The Shame–Humility–Guilt–Regret Continuum" to help them identify the emotion and determine a course of action to deal with it. As described earlier, toxic shame is not helpful in any way, so the first goal for the patient is to change her perspective cognitively. Once the patient cognitively understands the source of the shame or the distortion embedded in it, she can begin to change the experience of shame. This can be difficult because shame generally begins in childhood and may be deeply wired in the brain. Mindfulness and acceptance and commitment therapy (ACT) strategies teach people to increase awareness of the shame and shift to a different emotional state. I will say more about how to use these strategies in the next chapter.

If the shame is extremely pervasive, I find it useful to recommend a *3-minute-per-day mindfulness practice.* The patient is instructed to spend 3 minutes a day in thoughts that are inconsistent with the pervasive shame, such as, "It wasn't my fault; I did the best that I could; I am worthy of self-care," and so on. These thoughts can be written out ahead of time based on the specific history and needs of the patient. Eventually, the goal is for the patient to be able to consider what she needs to "hear" for each particular day. I tell patients that by doing this they will be re-wiring their brain. They will be using the prefrontal lobes during this practice, thus bringing the new thoughts to the forefront of their mind (literally). If they express trouble believing the thoughts, I simply encourage them that they will eventually "teach" their brain to believe the thoughts through this practice. Once the new thoughts are brought to the forefront of their mind, they are much more likely to be repeated throughout the day.

Ego States

One useful way to help clients understand their capacity for ambivalence is by using the concept of ego states described fully in Chapter 2. I explain to clients my model for understanding ego states using the terms *child, adolescent,* and *adult* and relate this to brain and cognitive development. One client told me that she didn't like the idea of an inner child and couldn't relate to the concept, so I explained that I was using that concept to identify all the experiences and learning that was stored in the part of her brain that was most active during her early years. This made sense to her, and then I was able to continue using language and strategies related to inner child concepts.

When teaching clients about the concept of ego states I ask them to imagine being vulnerable with someone and then getting criticized, such as when asking for a favor and being told, "You're too needy." Then I ask them how *old* they feel when imagining this event. They will often respond with an age before 10. Similarly if they're talking about being nervous at social events because they believe no one will like them and I ask how old they feel, they will often choose an age during adolescence. In contrast, if I ask them to imagine that someone accidentally cut themselves and they hurried to help, followed by the question of how old they feel, they usually will say something like their current age. By pondering these questions, clients can usually identify huge shifts in the thoughts, feelings, and action urges in these scenarios. Although still the same person, they can exhibit widely varying responses.

Regarding the child ego state, I explain that due to the limits of cognitive ability at this age, children are extremely vulnerable to what is happening around them. I explain that the brain is primarily learning through association without the capacity to evaluate this learning. I tell the story about teaching my child to name items as he was learning to talk. One day he brought me a flower that had died, and he called it "pretty flower." It was only then that I realized I had always said those two words together, and he had "learned" that they were one word as in *prettyflower*. Similarly, associations can be made, such as mom being very anxious when the child is crying, which can later be developed into a rule such as "don't show emotion." I also explain how shame may be a strong component of this ego state as children are assuming responsibility (egocentricity) for negative things that have happened.

On the other hand, the child ego state contains a strong ability and need to connect to others even at their own expense. Survival for babies and young children is dependent on connection to an adult; thus, we are hardwired to connect at almost any cost. We often discuss how the conflict between inaccurate learning about self and the development of shame coupled with the powerful need for connection often result in crippling ambivalence.

In teaching clients about their adolescent ego state, I focus on the rules and beliefs that have been formed and wired during the time the person was developing the capacity to use her posterior cerebral cortex. As in the preceding example, the child sensed that mom calmed down when she wasn't crying. As the child developed, she was able to start understanding the cause and effect rather than just the associations, which helped the child develop rules for surviving in her unique environment. I teach my clients that their rules made sense at one time but that it may be time to start reevaluating their usefulness going forward. I suggest that my clients increase awareness of rules by noticing when their thoughts are characterized by "should" or "never." It is useful at this point also to educate the client about how these rules have been interwoven into a narrative that guides them, sometimes very ineffectively, through life. Appendix A features a beliefs checklist that can be useful in helping clients increase awareness of beliefs and rules that were formed during this age.

Narratives are hard to change, as they have made very strong neural pathways in our brains relative to the number of times they have been repeated in our thoughts. I explain this to patients when they say they can't believe affirmations. I say, "Of course you can't yet, due to your previously formed neural pathways, but you wouldn't want an adolescent telling you what to believe and how to live, would you? Maybe it's time to tell that adolescent part of you a new story."

Finally, I teach my clients that the adult ego state is the part of the brain that can be used to enable them to heal from early wounds and to reevaluate faulty learning. I teach them about executive functioning aspects of the prefrontal lobes and describe how this part of the brain isn't even fully developed until about age 25. The adult ego state is analogous to the concept of wise mind, which clients can intuitively grasp by considering the type of advice they would give someone else. For instance, if a person has learned to hide emotions from others and I ask her if she'd give that advice to her best friend, she will usually say, "Of course not!" This enables me to point out that their child or adolescent ego state must be in conflict with their adult ego state causing the experience of ambivalence. "What would the wisest most self-confident person do with a dilemma like this?" The act of pondering the question to formulate an answer requires using the prefrontal lobes and thus developing and accessing an adult ego state. Additionally, I often use the empty chair technique described in Chapter 6 to help them experientially understand the process of learning to use their adult ego state effectively.

Conclusion

In summary, there are many benefits of spending adequate time on educating clients in these constructs. First, it will enable them to make sense of themselves. It also makes it easier to address difficult subjects as they arise. Thus, instead of saying to a client "Stop acting like a child," you can ask in a caring way, "What does the child part of you need right now from the wise, adult part?" Finally, this common language will provide a backdrop as you move through the stages of treatment focused on harnessing and resolving pathological ambivalence.

Chapter 6: Harnessing and Resolving Pathological Ambivalence

In Chapter 5, I presented the need to conduct assessment and provide education early in the treatment process. This can generally occur in two to three sessions, after which the therapist and client have a common language to use as they work through ambivalence toward change. For a discussion of using treatment plans and contracts, see Appendix B. This chapter focuses on specific techniques that have the potential for creating change quickly.

There are two overarching strategic mechanisms used when harnessing and resolving pathological ambivalence. The first group of strategies encourages the client to recognize his ambivalence and reflect on the dialectics involved, including the wisdom related to both sides of his dilemmas. These techniques are what I conceptualize as *teasing-apart* strategies, which encourage the patient to study both sides of the ambivalence with some detail. These strategies enable the client to challenge her own status quo. After the patient has increased awareness of the parts of her ambivalence, she will need to learn ways to harness the wisdom from both sides. Thus, the second group of skills discussed is devoted to *reintegrating* the parts or pulling them back together in a new way.

Strategies for Challenging the Status Quo

When people are struggling with pathological ambivalence, they often are unaware that they possess wisdom and fallacy on both sides of the problem and are generally stuck trying to determine which way to go. An ambivalent patient has a strong need to maintain the status quo, that is, to continue to believe and to act in ways that are familiar and habitual. This need is in direct conflict with her wish for change. The therapist facilitates expanding the patient's awareness to fully recognize that there are two sides with differing needs.

The following strategies encourage the patient to notice, when talking from only one side of his ambivalence, that there is actually another side to the story. To implement these methods to the fullest, keep in mind that all people have parts of which we may have varying degrees of awareness. This will be particularly helpful when you feel like disagreeing with something that the client has just said.

Exploring Polarities

Facilitating confusion. One way to help a patient see both sides is to create some confusion. If seemingly contradictory behavior is pointed out to the patient, she may initially feel a little confused. This observation may help facilitate some confusion about her habitual beliefs. As described in Chapter 4 in the context of Erickson's Confusion Technique (Erickson, Rossi, & Rossi, 1976), it is often through confusion that things can begin to shift. For instance, the therapist might say, "You talk about how meaningful our sessions are, but you often come in late. I'm wondering if there is a small part of you that is hesitant about something that might happen here." It is best to wait and see if the client has some insight about this, but if not, you might make a guess such as, "I'm wondering if a small part of you is afraid that I'll be judgmental." The guess would be based on what you already know from your work with this person or from his history. This is like Alfred Adler's concept of spitting in the soup (Mozak, 1985) in that he will never be able to say how meaningful the session is without contemplating the fact that he comes late.

Is there any other part of you that …? Often people will continue to maintain a previously formed belief even in the face of overwhelming contradictory evidence. I have worked with several Olympic athletes who continually struggled with beliefs that they weren't good enough. Their accomplishments were extraordinary, yet the belief persisted. One of these women, whom I'll refer to as Sylvia, had reported abuse growing up and had a learning disability. She had grown up believing that she was bad *and* stupid. Any attempt to get her to change her mind by recognizing her accomplishments was useless. If I were to tell her that she wasn't bad, for instance, she would simply begin thinking about all the reasons that she believed that she *was* bad. If I pointed out her accomplishments, she would say, "I know, I'm so stupid for thinking this way!" No matter which way I went, she went to thoughts of bad or stupid. We were obviously stuck.

One day she was talking about being unable to assert herself in a situation at work and related it to feeling that she didn't have a right to make the request. Instead of trying to convince her that she had every right to make the request, I simply asked her, "Is there any small part of you that feels differently?" In this way, I helped her to engage her own ambivalence rather than trigger a power struggle by advising her to be more assertive. She could sense a small part of herself that had always wanted to say that what had happened in her past wasn't her fault. It was as if there was a tiny spark of truth inside that needed oxygen so that the flame could grow.

I asked her to tell me more (adding oxygen) about the part of her that wanted to say it wasn't her fault. In a small, quiet voice, she did. We worked hard on putting lots of words to these thoughts and feelings so that she could begin creating new pathways in her brain. Now she had other thoughts that could, over time, compete with the well-worn thoughts of being bad and dumb.

Notice current self-care behaviors. Lori was riddled with shame. She engaged in many self-destructive behaviors and did not believe she was worthy of self-care. She had felt neglected as a child and had developed beliefs about herself that were extremely resistant to change. She could not bring herself to say even the simplest affirmation despite her expressed intention to change her behaviors. Because of these beliefs, it seemed impossible for her to even begin to decrease the self-destructive behaviors. In addition to more serious behaviors, she drank Diet Coke all day long. She already had done significant damage to her teeth due to chronic purging, and her dentist had warned her against drinking soda. When I asked her why she drank so much Diet Coke, she said that she liked the flavor. I "yes-butted" her (not generally an effective therapeutic strategy) by reminding her of the damage it was doing to her body and encouraging her to at least cut back. Predictably, that changed nothing.

It occurred to me that although this was an unhealthy behavior, it also had an element of self-care involved in that she was giving herself something she enjoyed. Rather than completely focusing on decreasing this behavior, I presented her with a choice, which created a dilemma for her. I suggested that she focus only on this one behavior for a week without necessarily trying to change it. She was willing, since it seemed so minor compared with the other behaviors we were trying to decrease. I pointed out that it was necessary for her body to have water (to which she intellectually agreed) and additionally that she drank Diet Coke because she deserved to have something that she wanted. When she started to object to the idea that she deserved it, I simply said, "Then drink water instead." Of course, she responded that she liked Diet Coke better. So we agreed that both were true; that she wanted to have something that she liked even though she didn't believe that she deserved it.

I then suggested that each time she had a Diet Coke, she acknowledge to herself that she was engaging in self-care because she was giving herself something she liked. She would say to herself every time she had a Diet Coke, "I deserve to have what I want." I added that if she couldn't acknowledge it as self-care, then she would simply have water instead. She agreed to this challenge. She now had a dilemma in that she had to acknowledge self-care regardless of whether she drank soda or water. I associated the unhealthy behavior (Coke) rather than the healthy behavior (water) with the concept of deserving because it was likely to occur more frequently. Simultaneously, if she couldn't bring herself to acknowledge that she was deserving of self-care, then her body got the water that, of course, was self-care. It was a win–win. Notice that this has elements of spitting in the soup, since now she had to associate Diet Coke with doing something nice for herself, which she was loath to acknowledge.

Highlighting Internal Dilemmas

Often when people are ambivalent regarding change, they are focused more on external causes for the dilemma. In these cases, it is helpful to point out that the dilemma is *their* dilemma because it is occurring in their life rather than between themselves and another person.

Court-ordered therapy. For instance, even when a person is court-ordered to be in therapy, he has the dilemma of how to respond to the situation. On the one hand, he isn't interested in therapy because someone else is causing it to happen. On the other hand, he must decide what to do with the time while he's there. John found himself in this situation after being court-ordered to therapy at a drug and alcohol center for repeated DUIs. He talked about how boring it was to have to come to therapy sessions. I initially tried to engage John by asking lots of questions (an example of my taking too much responsibility), then I tried sitting in silence with John (an example of my not taking enough responsibility). Either endeavor on my part ended up feeling like a power struggle.

Eventually, I handed the dilemma back to John in a way that helped him increase awareness of the power he still had to choose. "I see you have a dilemma in that you wouldn't choose to be here on your own, but you *are* here and must choose how to spend your time." In this way, I was not trying to make anything happen, but instead simply observing the obvious dilemma and then waiting to see what John chose to do.

John responded to this by stating, "Well, I definitely don't want to talk about my childhood!" I chuckled and asked him what kinds of things he usually did when he was bored, and he suggested that we just play cards. Guess who started spontaneously to talk about his childhood a couple of weeks later? By playing cards with John, I actually was expressing indifference to how we spent our time and to what we achieved, while simultaneously expressing interest in him as a person. By removing myself from the power struggle, John felt free to do whatever he truly wanted to do with the time, which eventually resulted in talking about his childhood. I believe that unconsciously, he wanted very much to talk about his childhood (but had internal rules against doing so), which is why he deliberately stated that he didn't want to. You can't always assume that clients are subconsciously telling you the exact opposite of what they want, but the beauty of these techniques is that you don't have to know. You present the dilemma to the patient and see where he takes it.

Active listening. I credit Carkhuff's (1972) active listening techniques with providing the foundation for staying out of power struggles with my early patients. Active listening is often considered as just a basic skill for building rapport in psychotherapy. But many clinicians do not realize that reflecting the client's own words can be an amazing tool for helping people quickly recognize the reason that they are feeling stuck or that they are, in fact, ambivalent.

For example, during a recent therapy group meeting, one member noted that she was afraid to fully recover from her eating disorder because she didn't want to have to experience the feelings her eating disorder allowed her to avoid. Instead of logically pointing out the problems associated with an eating disorder, I responded, "So *you feel* afraid to recover *because you can't yet believe* that you can manage hurtful feelings without your eating disorder." I didn't take either side, just reflected. She looked at me as if I'd just performed magic and said, "Wow, it's like you're in my mind!" She added, "I guess I'm going to have to find other ways to manage my feelings."

Active listening skills offer a unique way of empowering clients to hear themselves out loud and to access their own wisdom. A fully formed Carkhuffian statement utilizes a sentence map: "You feel _____ because you _____, but you can't _____." For example, "So you feel lonely and frustrated because you want to meet people but you can't get over your anxiety about being judged." Or "You feel torn because you want meaningful relationships but you can't believe that people won't hurt you in the long run."

This type of active listening requires no interpretation or advice. Simply reflect the client's own words. It's hard for people to be resistant or in denial when it comes to their own words. The last part of the sentence map points to what needs to be change, such as anxiety about being judged.

Concept of Multiple Motives

Whenever someone is stuck with an either/or question, I am inclined to suggest that it is both. I use the example of a kiss. When we kiss someone, is our motive to kiss or to be kissed? It's both! We don't have to decide which motive is true, and one doesn't discount the other. Individuals with pathological ambivalence often get bogged down with trying to figure out which of two motives is real or appropriate, and they may even feel shame over one of the motives.

In my work with people with eating disorders, I have often heard parents say that they don't know if their daughter has a real eating disorder or is just trying to get attention. I respond with something like,

"What if it's both? It's likely that she is using eating disorder symptoms to manage something that needs attending to."

Marsha's story illustrates multiple motives in another context. Marsha was getting ready to celebrate her father's birthday. She had decided several months earlier that she would take him to dinner and had already invited him. In the meantime, she had begun working in therapy on her perfectionism. She was becoming increasingly aware of how his personality style had affected the development of her perfectionism and was feeling some anger about this. As her therapist, I was tempted to encourage her to express her anger directly to her father in an endeavor of using her voice, so to speak. She was also in group therapy where other group members were enthusiastically encouraging her to use her voice as well.

As the birthday dinner drew closer, however, she began to experience ambivalence about seeing her father at all. She was able to talk about her two conflicting motives: the part of her that wanted to honor her father's birthday, and the part of her that wanted to honor her voice. She was stuck because she felt that whatever she did, she would be disappointing someone (me and group members or her father, as well as each part of herself).

As we discussed the dilemma, she began to accept that both motives were valid. This enabled her to get unstuck and to determine a course of action. She decided that although she was angry with her father, she also still loved him and decided to focus on one part of her feelings at a time. During the birthday dinner, she focused on all the things she loved about her father and then asked him to meet her on a different day for coffee to discuss her other feelings. In this way, she acknowledged both sides of her ambivalence without denying either.

Shifting Ego States

What age do you feel? Another way to conceptualize ambivalence is through the concept of ego states, as described in Chapter 2. Naomi was struggling with the belief that she could never get over her depression. She was telling herself that she had been going through this for so long that she had lost hope that it would ever be different. She was afraid that I was going to give up on her as well. She told herself things like she was not going to be cared for, that she couldn't trust others and that she was better off alone. As she said these things, she sounded more angry and aggressive than depressed. Then she abruptly shifted gears, and in a much quieter voice stated that she was really trying hard and wanted things to be better. She was tired of her self-sabotaging behaviors. These words sounded wise, but the tone was more like that of a child.

In the conceptual framework of ego states, at the beginning of this conversation, Naomi was in an adolescent ego state, which almost bullied her into distrust of and anger toward others. Then she shifted to a child ego state, which desperately wanted connection and acceptance. These two ego states had opposing fears and goals which kept her confused and pathologically ambivalent.

After educating Naomi about ego states, we had the following conversation:

> **T:** How old does the part of you feel that tells you that you can't trust anyone?
> **N:** It seems real big and mean but if I really think about it (here she's using prefrontal lobes), I'd say about 14 years old.
> **T:** What is that part most afraid of if you don't do what she says?
> **N:** That I'll get even more depressed because I'll get hurt.
> **T:** When you were saying that you were trying real hard and wanted to get better, how old did you feel?
> **N:** About 4 years old.
> **T:** So what was that 4-year-old feeling?
> **N:** Afraid that my treatment team would send me away.
> **T:** So I wonder if you can step back and think about the wisdom and fallacy that each of those parts experiences?

Naomi learned to use her adult ego state (which is the same as using an observing mind, prefrontal lobes, wise mind, etc.) to reflect on these two younger parts of herself. She could see why the adolescent part of her had developed these rules and scripts from childhood and how they had been adaptive at one point. She saw that by telling herself these things years ago in the context of her early experiences, she had been better able to manage disappointment or depression. As she talked, she began to recognize, however, that the very rules that had helped her previously were now causing the depression to worsen. While she discussed this, I observed that she was calmer and that her tone of voice sounded strong but not aggressive, so I asked her how old she felt as she considered these things. She answered, "I feel about my age now." In future conversations with Naomi when she seemed to be in a child or adolescent ego state, I would ask her if she could get in touch with her adult self. Over time she could validate that both parts of her ambivalence had some wisdom and that she could find a path toward change that took both into account. She was able to identify goals about which both parts of her could agree. One such goal was to, with caution, look for people she could trust and connect with. It should be noted that, as a team, we had been neglecting the adolescent's fear each time we tried to support the child part that wanted to trust people. The art of psychotherapy is being able to simultaneously address the fear on both sides.

This type of conversation, by the way, is exactly the way I would talk with someone who has dissociative identity disorder (DID). Although Naomi didn't have DID, she did have an underdeveloped adult ego state and strongly formed child and adolescent ego states that were not participating together well.

What do you need to hear yourself say? Another strategy that helps patients recognize their ambivalence and resolve it via their own wisdom (adult ego state) is to ask them to make grounding statements: what they need to hear themselves say to reduce anxiety. We use this technique at Atlanta Center for Eating Disorders (ACE) during meal process groups, in which patients practice mindfully eating what their body needs. People in these groups have varying reasons to struggle with this. For instance, one person may feel that if she limits herself to eating only what's on her plate, she will feel deprived and restricted (child ego state), while another patient might feel that she doesn't deserve to eat everything on her plate (adolescent ego state).

In eliciting grounding statements. I ask participants to consider what they need to hear themselves say to decrease their anxiety about eating, and then to say it out loud. In this way, they are learning to speak from the adult ego state to the child or adolescent ego state. Examples of grounding statements are "my body needs this food" or "I'm not restricting myself because I will eat again in just a few hours." This helps avoid the power struggle that often occurs when the therapist tries to convince the patients of these truths, and it has more meaning in that patients are putting it in their own words based on their own experience in the moment. Those who are suffering with extreme ambivalence often hate doing these grounding statements because they have so much resistance to using their healthy or wise voice. To these patients, I suggest that they state what someone else in their position would need to hear even if they don't yet believe it for themselves.

In individual therapy, when I am tempted to confront a client's irrational belief, I first try to ask clients, "What do you need to hear yourself say right now that would be reassuring in some way?" By thinking about how to answer this question, they must focus inward using the prefrontal lobes. If necessary, I can counteract their irrational beliefs lending them, in a sense, my prefrontal lobes. Obviously, however, they can't carry my brain around with them so they must learn to do this for themselves in the moment, using mindfulness skills. When asked this question, Anja, who struggled with perfectionism, paused and then said, "I guess I need to hear that it's okay if I make a B sometimes." Of course, this is what I had wanted to say to her, but when something is fairly obvious yet the client is resisting the truth, it doesn't help for us to point out the obvious. Clients needs to experience themselves reaching for the truth internally and explore the narratives that make seeing the obvious more difficult. Anja's narrative was that people would reject her if she wasn't perfect.

The Power of Group Therapy

Group therapy is an extremely powerful method for working with pathological ambivalence. In fact, I believe it is more powerful than individual therapy for these individuals.

The rest of the story. Doing group therapy enables the therapist to see the client in a setting that more closely approximates the clients' real world. I had been working with Heather for several months in individual therapy, during which she talked about how others had mistreated her or hurt her feelings and about her lack of friends. Given her issues, I thought that an interpersonal group would be good for her. In group, it was like she was a different person. I saw that she was extremely sensitive to feedback and would react with silence and anger even when it was well intentioned. It became clear that some of her defenses, which I hadn't seen in individual therapy, were causing the rejection that she had been telling me about before being in the group. I realized that by seeing her interact with others, I was seeing the *rest of the story*, which enabled me to treat her more effectively.

Wisdom for others. Another advantage of group therapy is the wisdom that people give and receive from each other. Frequently, when people are ambivalent, they can offer wisdom to others that they can't give themselves (an endeavor that can't happen in individual therapy). This is a common occurrence in group therapy and can be pointed out to challenge the status quo within the individual. In one group in which members were helping each other plan for potential obstacles that they might encounter during the weekend, one member, Kathy, was complaining about her boyfriend. She negated each person's suggestion until one person said, "It seems that you really don't want any help right now." We moved on. Over the course of the group, Kathy gave excellent advice to others. I sensed that it was becoming apparent to everyone that she could offer help to others but had difficulty receiving it. So, I said in a voice that I hoped sounded shaman-like, "She who has great wisdom for others ..." Before I could even finish the sentence, Kathy said, "I know, I can't take it for myself." She laughed and then came up with a strategy for her weekend.

Use of Humor

When used appropriately, humor can be an effective therapeutic tool. In the preceding example of Kathy, when I used my funny voice to make a potentially serious observation, it softened the blow and enabled Kathy to laugh at herself as well. Using humor lets the patient see that you still are connected and that whatever is happening isn't the end of the world. It also can throw patients off guard when they are least expecting it.

Noah was a 17-year-old brought to ACE for an assessment of a possible eating disorder. He had been purging and was not doing well in school. As part of the assessment, Noah sat at a computer monitor and answered a lengthy questionnaire. He was so visibly angry about being brought to the assessment that the intake coordinator and the intern who was assisting me warned that I was going to have my hands full with this one. Feeling a bit of dread, I sat down to read his assessment before meeting with him. His answers were full of sarcastic humor, stating clearly that he wasn't taking the assessment seriously and he did not want to be there. However, I recognized just enough wisdom in his answers that I considered he wanted to be understood but didn't believe it would happen here.

I knew that he would expect me to scold him for not taking the assessment seriously, but I could see that this kid had intelligence and a quick wit. So, when I met him, I told him this was the most fun I had ever had reading an assessment questionnaire (which it was). I added that I had been eager to meet him because I love his type of humor. It threw him off a little, but also made him feel very accepted that I got his humor.

Sixteen-year-old Anaya came for an assessment and though it was of her own choice, she seemed very ambivalent. I asked her how she felt about doing the assessment, to which she answered, "I can't believe that you actually asked me how I feel about being here. That is the most stereotyped question that a therapist could say! Did you really ask me how do I feel?"

My first reaction was shock at her rudeness, but I was also impressed by the strength of her presence for such a young girl. After a pause while my shock shifted, I said with a chuckle and a smile, "Gosh, I love your snarkiness." Then she said with a sheepish grin, "Yea, I can be really snarky." The tone of the entire session then shifted.

Another patient I worked with in group therapy had been seriously neglected in her childhood and was filled with self-loathing. Jennifer expressed this self-loathing by looking disinterested and disapproving of others. She wouldn't let people get close to her and the message she gave off was that everyone and everything was stupid. After being gone for a week on vacation, I came into group a few minutes early, and she was in there with one or two other people. The others welcomed me back, but Jennifer did not make eye contact. As I walked by her to open some blinds, I said, "Don't even sit there not making eye contact and pretend that you didn't miss me! I know better!" She couldn't help but smile and shake her head at the outrageous things that could come out of my mouth. In this way, I gave her feedback about her lack of eye contact but was able to make her laugh rather than present it as a problem that she had to work on.

Shima was in a narrative group that I was leading. I asked her if she could identify with any of the beliefs listed on a worksheet we were using (see Appendix A) and how this might relate to her eating disorder. She paused and said that she wasn't sure she had an eating disorder. Shima was in a residential program and apparently was resisting the diagnosis, although it had been thoroughly explained to her. I just said, "Oh, okay," and moved on. Later in the group, she related to a script that mistakes are fatal. I leaned over and muttered, "By the way, perfectionism is linked to developing eating disorders. Not with you I'm sure, …just saying." Smiling, she responded, "Yeah, not with me." Then she talked about how she had interpreted some of her parent's behavior as implying that she needed to be perfect. She began to explore this. At the end of the group, I asked her if she was beginning to feel crazy yet, She replied that she kind of was, and I said "Then my job here is done." She laughed, but then in all seriousness I assured her that as she continued in recovery, she would actually feel less crazy and begin to know that she made sense. I could have talked with her about her denial of her symptoms, which would have probably made her feel defensive. Instead, I chose to be patient, wait for an opening, and then use humor. All of this was said with a playful smile, and she responded playfully as well.

Although humor can be powerful, it can also backfire. It is important when using any therapeutic strategy that it fits you as a person and that the client is likely to interpret it as humor. I think when using this strategy, you need to genuinely be feeling affection and acceptance toward the client, and, as with any strategy, you should always use it with specific intent.

Motivational Interviewing

Psychologist Linda Sobell has used motivational interviewing (MI) for individuals with addiction problems. She and her husband have written an extremely comprehensive, yet easy to use and understand, summary of MI strategies and the related questions (Sobell & Sobell, 2008). I highly recommend going over the questions several times so that they will be on your mind whenever you are sitting with clients.

The beauty of MI is that it facilitates a collaborative relationship between the client and the therapist, communicating to the client that his or her answers and wisdom are within. The therapist functions more like a tour guide, suggesting that the client look to the left and then to the right to see what can be seen—but doesn't see it for them. In addition to the open-ended questions of MI, there are two strategies I find most helpful when dealing with pathological ambivalence: values clarification and developing discrepancies.

Values clarification. Values can be defined as guiding principles that enable us to acknowledge that which is important to us. These principles, then, should affect our behavior and help us build the life that we would want to live. The problem occurs when we have competing beliefs, fears, or scripts that would produce behaviors that are opposed to our values—for example, when a person places a high value on relationships but also has a fear of rejection.

Brooke was keenly aware of her value of building relationships and being a good, loyal friend. However, she also had a subtle and long-held fear of rejection, which caused her to be somewhat guarded around her friends. She was always available to help them but rarely asked for help herself. The one-sided nature of these relationships eventually affected the depth of them. Brooke was aware of her value as a good friend and her fear of rejection but was not fully aware of how her fear interfered with her value. It can be helpful, therefore, to help people clarify the most important values they hold.

Once values are clarified and prioritized, the patient can learn to ask herself, "How is what I'm doing now supporting or interfering with one of my values?" I tell people that if they don't live according to their own values, they will eventually spring a leak. Again, this is a way to avoid a power struggle because the therapist is not suggesting to the patient what the value should be, but rather simply pointing out discrepancies between behaviors and values. These discrepancies usually result from early scripts formed in childhood, as in the case of Brooke's fear of being rejected.

Steps in values clarification (worksheet can be found on Mindtools .com):

Step 1: Analyze times when you feel happiest.

Step 2: Identify the times when you are most proud.

Step 3: Identify times when you are most fulfilled and satisfied.

Step 4: Determine your top values.

In this step, it is helpful to use a comprehensive list of values to choose from, such as the Core Values List (see http://corevalueslist.com/).

It can become especially confusing when a person's ambivalence is occurring due to competing values—for example, the value of spending time with family versus the value of being successful at work. Developing a values hierarchy can help people make decisions in the context of competing values.

David excelled on the job and had moved up quickly in his company. He valued being a dependable, hard worker. When he and his wife had children, he valued being a good father. He was unaware, though, of how often he made decisions about his time based on his good employee value rather than his good father value. When asked which he would rank higher, he quickly responded that being a good father was more important. This discrepancy was pointed out so that he could become more conscious of living according to his values in the order of importance to him.

In the style of Columbo, the therapist might say something like, "I'm confused in that you say being a good father is the higher value, but you work many late nights. Can we talk about how you actually make decisions about how to spend your time?"

Develop discrepancy. Once the client has identified and clarified his values, you can help him recognize discrepancies between competing values or between the current lifestyle and his vision for the future. It is helpful to separate the behavior from the person and help him explore how important personal goals (e.g., good health, marital happiness, financial success) are being undermined by problematic behaviors. Once a client begins to understand how the consequences or potential consequences of current behavior conflict with significant personal values, motivation for change will increase.

Four other useful techniques for challenging the patient's desire to maintain the status quo are as examining the pros and cons, examining exceptions to the problem, the Miracle Question, and gestalt body work. Descriptions of these strategies can be found in Appendix D.

Whereas the strategies previously described were focused on enabling a client to see the duality or multiplicity in their personality, the strategies in the next section are focused on ways to integrate the parts into a well-functioning whole. Often I will use a technique that challenges the status quo such as those described earlier in the chapter, followed immediately by an integration technique in the same session.

Integrating Splits—While Staying Out of Them

When people are struggling with pathological ambivalence, it is important that the therapist facilitate a process through which they generate their own form of integration and resolutions. This is not to say that the person no longer has parts, since personality is inherently made up of parts, but after resolving ambivalence, the parts to our personality work more cooperatively toward the same goals. The first three techniques have in common the goal of integrating ego states by accessing wise mind. The next three are focused on general strategies for integration.

Gestalt Empty Chair

This technique is typically used to help the client work through interpersonal issues, but I use it for addressing *intra*personal splits. There are at least three benefits of using the empty chair technique. First, it reduces power struggles between the therapist and client. When I realize that I've gotten into a power struggle with a client, such as when I find myself trying to persuade them that change is possible or good for them, the empty chair technique can interrupt this unhelpful interaction.

Second, the empty chair technique increases insight into sources of ambivalence and the wisdom on each side, especially when a client says something like, I'm torn, I can't decide, I don't know which is right, I'm confused about which I want, or I'm just waffling, or if she is speaking from just one part of her ambivalence. Third, it facilitates and enables problem solving.

When introducing the empty chair technique I ask, "Would you be willing to try an experiment with me? It's a little odd but it can be very revealing." I structure the exercise by reviewing the concept of parts or ego states, if needed, and by normalizing the experience of ambivalence. I then explain that people often have ambivalence and that ambivalent thoughts can be like a ping-pong game just going back and forth incessantly in their mind. The goal, then, is to take the conversation out of their head and into the room to help them see it more clearly and understand why they are stuck.

Next, the client is instructed to describe the ambivalence in terms of "one part of me wants or thinks ... while another part wants or thinks ...." I explain that I am going to facilitate a conversation between the two parts while the patient is sitting in one chair which is positioned across from an empty chair. The client will choose which part she wants to speak first, and when that part is finished, she will then move to the other chair to allow the other side to speak. I am very active as a "coach" during this exercise, helping the person to avoid switching sides unknowingly and providing sentence stems as needed to facilitate a thorough expression of both sides. I recommend allowing them to start with whatever he'd like to say and then providing sentence stems when he pauses. The sentence stems I use most commonly are the following:

1. What you don't understand ...
2. When you tell me _____, I feel ...
3. What I wish you'd do differently ...
4. When you say/do that, it reminds me of (what or whom?) ...
5. If I listen to you, I'm afraid that ...
6. I understand that you feel ...

This exercise can be very intense and eye-opening and can be done in individual or group therapy settings. It is my opinion that in most cases of pathological ambivalence, the two parts speaking are a child and an adolescent ego state. Often the adolescent ego state sounds authoritative and adult-like because it was patterned after early caregivers, but the energy that motivates this part is generally anxiety rather than the calmer energy of the adult ego state. When the adolescent part is operating, the fears, core beliefs, and narrative by which they live are being expressed. When the child part is most present, the person's innermost desires and wishes are being expressed.

When a person is struggling with pathological ambivalence, the wise mind (aka adult ego state, observing self or nurturing parent part) has not been accessed, which is why the person has not found a resolution to the ambivalence. The client needs to be encouraged to see that both parts are "younger" (that is, ego states formed at earlier ages) and that they probably correspond with beliefs and feelings that they had while growing up. Each of these beliefs and feelings contains some wisdom and some fallacy.

Therefore, I have added a third step, to enable the client to access the adult ego state. After both sides have thoroughly expressed themselves (which may take changing chairs more than once), I suggest that there has been a third chair in the room in which the wisest part of them has been sitting. This part knows exactly why each of the younger parts feels and thinks the way they do and this wiser, older part knows the way out of the dilemma. I then ask the client to talk about what this wise part would say to each "younger" part to validate, reassure, and advise them. In doing this part of the exercise, the individual will be using the prefrontal lobes (or wise mind) to access the wisdom from both the emotional and rational minds.

The following is an example of an empty chair exercise I used in the context of group therapy. Lauren was in her late 20s, was chronically depressed, suffered with severe feelings of shame, and expressed hopelessness that things would ever improve. She described her father when growing up as fun to be with but absent due to his multiple affairs and her mother as emotionally cut off. Lauren had a longtime boyfriend who was an addict but had been clean for more than a year. She had just found out that he had been using again for about a month. On this particular day, she was struggling with a decision about whether to break up with him. As she talked about her sense of betrayal, the group was quick to support her in breaking up with him; however, she seemed to be resistant to making a decision. After describing her dilemma, she agreed to the empty chair exercise and chose to allow the part of her that did not want to break up with him to speak first.

Lauren: I don't want to break up with him because he's all I have. It's not that big a deal that he had a slip, it happens to everyone. If you [*speaking to the other part of her in the empty chair*] break up with him, you will be alone and even more depressed. You should take into account his feelings and not be so selfish.

T: When you tell me that I should break up with him, I feel …

Lauren: When you tell me that I should break up with him, I feel mad because you are naïve and you always want things your way and you act like the world should be a perfect place. You dwell on the negative. You aren't even thinking about all the things he does for you. You can't make it in the world by yourself. [*This is a clear example of an adolescent part talking to a child part.*]

T: When you act that way, it reminds me of …

Lauren: When you act that way, it reminds me of when I was little and wishing that Dad would spend time with me. He didn't care about you when he was having affairs. You can't always have everything you want. You need to appreciate what you have rather than focus on your unhappiness. You won't find anyone better than him, and you'll be alone.

T: If I listen to you, I'm afraid that …

Lauren: If I listen to you and do break up with him, I'm afraid that I will become even more depressed and suicidal.

T: What I wish you'd do differently is …

Lauren: What I wish you'd do differently is accept that life is hard and stop being so depressed all the time. You need to toughen up!

T: What I wish you understood, that you just don't get, is …

Lauren: What I wish you understood is that I am trying to help you.

T: Is there anything else that this part of you wants to say to the part of you that wants to break up with him?

Lauren: No.

At this point, Lauren switched seats. She was instructed to get in touch with the part of her that wanted to break up with her boyfriend and to respond to what she had just heard the other part of her say.

Lauren: I need to break up with him because he was dishonest by trying to keep this a secret. He knows that I can't tolerate secrets. If he's keeping this a secret, then I don't have any idea what to trust. If he really loved you (speaking to the part sitting in the empty chair), he would have let you know that he was struggling. He knows that I can understand about a slip, but not about dishonesty.

T: When you tell me not to break up with him…

Lauren: When you tell me not to break up with him, I feel trapped, unimportant and weak. I feel like what I want or need doesn't matter.

T: If I do what you want …

Lauren: If I do what you want, I'm afraid that I will never truly feel important. I need to know that I'm strong and don't have to depend totally on someone else for my happiness.

T: What I wish you understood is …

Lauren: What I wish you understood is that I should have a right to my own expectations and to have my needs met.

T: When you don't validate that, it reminds me of …

Lauren: When you don't validate that, it reminds me of mom telling me to stop complaining and get over it. She was upset with dad too and would never let me talk about it. She just put up with it! [*long pause*] … I wonder if part of her wanted to leave him.

T: What I wish you'd do differently …

Lauren: What I wish you'd do differently is pay attention to my feelings every once in a while.

T: What you really don't understand is…

Lauren: What you really don't understand is that I have rights too, and I'd rather be alone than settle for less.

T: Is there anything else that this part of you would like to say to the other part?

Lauren: You talk to me so mean! If you want to help, you should start by treating me nicer.

At this point, the group leader asked for feedback from other group members, such as what wisdom and fallacy did they see in each side? Could they identify if either side was an adolescent or child ego state? The group members identified the part of Lauren that wanted to break up with her boyfriend as the child ego state. This part of her held much wisdom about deserving to get her needs met but was also inaccurate in assuming that if her boyfriend loved her, he wouldn't have used. That thought is an example of the egocentric ways that young children think. The part that wanted to stay with the boyfriend was the adolescent ego state, the part of her that had developed rules and beliefs about herself, relationships, and the world that were formed when she was growing up in a dysfunctional family system. However, this part of her also held wisdom about not dwelling on the negative and recognizing that life can be hard. It is important to note that there is wisdom on both sides, or the person wouldn't be ambivalent.

Next, the participant is asked to imagine that their adult self or wise-self had been listening to the entire conversation. This part of her understood exactly why each part felt the way it did and knew the way out of the dilemma.

> **T:** Can you validate some of what each part said and then decide on a course of action?
>
> **L:** *To the adolescent self:* I can see why you try to get me to accept "what is" rather than feel unhappy. That did help me cope when I was growing up. However, you try to motivate me to feel better by sounding just like mom. Now that I'm not stuck in that family environment, I can create a life for myself that is better than I had then. *To the child self:* Although you do need to accept that life is hard, you are right to express your feelings and prioritize your needs.
>
> **T:** What do you [*adult ego state*] need to do for each of them?
>
> **Lauren:** I need to let the adolescent part of me know that it is okay to have needs and wants, and that I will take over helping the child when she's disappointed. I need to tell her that she is loveable and that, although there's no real reason to believe she'll be alone, the most important thing is for her to know that she's worthy of being treated well. And I need to tell the child part of me that I will listen to her feelings but that when she is feeling hurt, I will not allow her to just stay in bed. I will help her manage her feelings so that the adolescent doesn't think she has to take over and try to talk her out of them.
>
> **T:** If you give these parts your wisdom, where does that lead you as far as dealing with your boyfriend?
>
> **Lauren:** I'm not sure what I'll do yet, but if I'm feeling stronger, I will be able to talk with him about his slip without feeling unlovable and afraid of being alone. I might even be more compassionate to him whether I stay or leave. If I'm stronger, I can see that his behavior is not a reflection on me but does affect me.... And be able to make a choice based on what's best for me now rather than on the fears I developed growing up.

This wisdom was within Lauren all the time, and she had been seen sharing advice like this to others. She had trouble taking her own advice because she was stuck trying to figure out which side of her was right.

By hearing out both sides of her dilemma with compassion and openness, she was able to apply her inherent wisdom to her own ambivalence.

There are so many things that I love about the empty chair exercise, not the least of which is that it is so easy! Other than the therapist throwing out a few sentence stems, the client does all the work. It is beautiful to sit back and watch the increased awareness, the "aha" moments and the wisdom just flow from the participant. I am always amazed at how fast we get to the crux of the matter and go places that I may have never known we needed to go. I think the biggest obstacle to using this technique is simply therapist inhibition. Therapists may feel that it's awkward or that the patient will feel funny about doing it. However, in my opinion, if the therapist is sold on the power of the technique and presents it with confidence, the client will generally go with it, maybe with a few giggles at first.

Although the majority of my clients agree to do the empty chair technique when I suggest it, there are some who are uncomfortable. Several other strategies, although generally not as powerful, can achieve similar results. These include split column journaling, guided imagery, and using self-portraits or photos. Descriptions and examples of how I've used them toward these goals in therapy can be found in Appendix E.

Letters to Self

Another journaling exercise that can help with integrating parts is writing a letter to another part of oneself. This helps clients gain understanding, empathy, and acceptance, as well as increase trust in themselves. It may seem strange to think that one part of me might not trust another part of me. However, in my work I encounter this with almost every client who is struggling with pathological ambivalence. The letter may be written from the wise adult to the child or adolescent and vice versa. I often give people a list of statements that may be helpful in generating the letter, telling them to use it only as a starting point and not to feel constricted in any way. The following are some of the common statements that I suggest.

Since it is the adolescent ego state that I conceptualize as holding the rules and beliefs from childhood, I often recommend writing a letter to this part from the adult, wise self. In this letter, the client is encouraged to validate the reasons that existed for developing the early beliefs. The following worksheet helps structure the letter. (A similar letter can be written to the child part as well but would have very different sentence stems.)

1. I understand that you believed …
2. Those beliefs used to make sense because …
3. I know that you were helping me by …
4. I appreciate how hard you worked to …
5. I don't want you to have to …
6. What I hope for you now is …
7. What I can do for you now is …

The following is paraphrased from a letter one of my patients wrote to her adolescent self.

Dear Adolescent,

You have been working so hard for so many years to earn approval. I understand that you grew up believing that you had to be perfect to please others. Because mom was so anxious, you felt like you had to be super responsible to decrease her stress. No matter how hard you tried, though, it never seemed to be enough because I've learned now that you can't be responsible for how someone else lives, and you can't change other people. Since you were trying to do something that is impossible, you believed that you were inadequate. That was a logical assumption based on an irrational belief. I appreciate how hard you worked and due to your hard work and caring of others, I have achieved a great deal. However, I wish that while you were growing up, someone had helped you realize that you were good enough already. In fact, you're pretty fantastic. I don't need you to try so hard anymore, in fact now it's making me too stressed and lonely. What I want for you now is to realize that I know how hard you tried and I don't need you to try so hard anymore. I don't need it because I've learned that some of what I try to do is impossible and unnecessary. I've learned now that people don't expect that out of me, I just assumed it back then. I will

make choices now for you about what needs to be done and what
can be left undone. I want you to rest now, knowing that I love
you and that you are inherently loveable.

Representative Objects

As patients begin to learn about and acknowledge their parts, you can teach them ways to become increasingly aware of their parts outside of the therapy office as well. Representative objects can create this increased mindfulness. With younger children, I present a basket of stuffed animals and ask them to pick one animal to represent one side of their ambivalence and another animal for the other. I often use these same stuffed animals with adults as well.

One 10-year-old client who had developed anorexia described fear about gaining weight but also was very distressed that she was upsetting her parents. She chose a small bear to be the part that was afraid of gaining weight and a bunny to represent the part that wanted to please her parents. She then let each talk to me. This was very similar to the empty chair exercise, and we sometimes shifted to placing one of the animals in the empty chair once she began to understand the process better. She named the two animals, and eventually chose a third animal, a giraffe, to represent herself as separate from the two that were arguing against each other. She was able to have the third animal speak to the other two with amazing wisdom for a 10-year-old. I let her take the stuffed animals home so that she could "play" with them, on the condition that she bring them back for her sessions. Whenever I recognized that she was speaking from the bear or bunny part of her, I'd ask her to tell me what the giraffe would say. I'd follow up her answer by asking her what the giraffe needed to do for the other part that was scared or mad, etc. I rarely had to give her advice or tell her what to do, because the giraffe already had that wisdom. Eventually when she had recovered from the eating disorder, I gave her the giraffe as a parting gift.

Compromise

One of the simplest ways to integrate splits is by creating a compromise. Whenever a client expresses an either/or dilemma, consider the possibility of a compromise between the two. Janet had not seen her parents for two years and was ambivalent about having a relationship with them. They called to say that they were coming through her town and wondered if they could spend the weekend with her. She was torn about whether to say yes or no. She could not imagine spending a weekend with them but also could not bring herself to say no. Assuming that there must be wisdom in each side of her dilemma, I asked if there was a compromise that would honor both sides of her dilemma. This led to her decision to offer her home for one night instead of the entire weekend. Sometimes, I educate my clients that if they are really stuck, it may be as simple as coming up with a mathematical average halfway between the two options. Although it may feel as if neither option is a perfect choice, it incorporates enough positive from both options that she is likely to find that she can actually make a decision. Compromises are generally achieved through understanding and harnessing the positive aspects of both sides of a dilemma.

Therapist's Dilemma

This strategy is helpful when the therapist is unsure about what to do next. It is very common for therapists to experience ambivalence when doing psychotherapy, so we need strategies for dealing with our own ambivalence. The wonderful thing about this approach is that not only does it take the burden off the therapist to decide what to do when ambivalent; it almost always empowers the patient to make a wise choice.

Jane, a 38-year-old mother of two, was talking to me about an upsetting conversation that she had had with her mom. She said with a very little girl voice, "When these things happen, I feel like no one understands or cares how I feel." I was torn. I sensed that she was indirectly asking me to tell her that I cared and understood, and I was tempted to do that. Also, she sure looked like she needed a hug and I think that hugs from therapists are a helpful intervention at times. However, it was hard for her to take care of herself emotionally, and I didn't want to become a substitute mom at the expense of her becoming more competent in taking care of herself. Anything that I can give or do for the patient is something that I would prefer them to do for themselves. I said, "as I think of that little girl part of you that feels so alone right now, I want to put my arm around her and tell her I understand and it's all going to be all right, but as I think of the adult part of you who often knows how to handle difficult situations, I want to step back and encourage her to figure this out. I'm ambivalent. Which do you need from me right now?"

She paused for a minute and I actually saw her facial features shift as her mental state changed. Before I asked my question, she had looked and sounded like a lonely and scared little girl. As she thought about her answer, her face seemed to relax and a sense of knowing seemed to come over her. She said, "That little girl needs a hug from me (herself)."

This simple intervention enabled many therapeutic processes. By asking her which response she most needed from me in this moment, I was relieved of the burden of making the decision and possibly making the wrong one. Additionally, as she pondered her response to my question, she had to switch from emotional mind to wise mind. This also enabled her to remember and consider her long-term goal, which was to feel more empowered and responsible for herself (adult ego state) rather than vulnerable to others to take care of her (child ego state). The fact that I offered a hug discouraged her from retreating to her common fear that no one really cares (a story that her adolescent part repeats to keep her from feeling disappointed). Finally, when a patient uses her adult self to comfort a child ego state, integration is occurring inside. The parts are working together for a common goal.

Had I only offered the reassurances and the hug, she may have felt a short-term comfort; however, she wouldn't have experienced the longer term empowerment of comforting herself. Had I gone quickly to encouraging her to comfort herself, before she was in wise mind, the emotional or child part of her may have felt rejected. With this use of my own ambivalence and knowing that she probably had wisdom on both sides, I really couldn't lose.

Not everyone is ready to do for themselves what they want you to do for them, even when presented with both options. Katie was in constant need of someone to reassure her that she was important; however, her need was so strong and so intense that there was nothing anyone could do to reassure her. It caused her to need to be in crisis. She could not believe that someone would care for her based on who she was; however, she would get a short-term sense of connectedness and worth when someone would help her out of a crisis. This pattern had resulted in multiple treatments over multiple years.

I educated Katie about what I perceived as her need to be in crisis to feel important. I also told her that every time someone helped her out of a crisis, it reinforced her original fear that she wasn't important otherwise and that I didn't want to be an accomplice in this experience.

I told her that the only way out of this pattern was for her to learn to care for herself when she was in crisis so that she could learn that others would care for her without the crisis. One day, she came in upset and seemingly in crisis. She said that she knew she was supposed to help herself but that she didn't want to, it just didn't seem to matter at all, and she didn't know if she could keep it up.

I told her I was torn. "There is a part of me that very much wants to tell you how important you are, how worthy you are of being loved. I want to work very hard to convince you of that. I want to give you a hug. There is another part of me that knows that all this has been tried before and I can't seem to convince you of your worth. I know that your only relief will come when you begin to give yourself this message. What do you think is the most important thing for me to do right now?"

She nodded at what I had said and paused and then said, "I just need a hug." The fact that she had to make the decision put her in a position of responsibility; asking to get her needs met directly rather than indirectly by trying to get me to prove that I cared about her. In this case, I was more than happy to give her a hug.

Two Truths

To help a patient cope with ambivalence, I point out that often there are two truths that exist in the same moment but that might call for very different actions. This is based on the concept of dialectics.

One beautiful, sunny spring day, I was driving in to work when I saw a woman gardening in her yard. I was filled with a sense of longing and envy and I said to myself, "I wish I could be gardening today." My mood immediately dropped. My wish couldn't be fulfilled. Now I felt frustrated as I was driving to work. All of this happened in an instant. I became mindful of how quickly my mood had shifted from contentment to discontent.

There were two truths operating at the same time. It is true that I would like to be gardening; however, it was also true that I was driving to a job that I loved and for which I was truly grateful. I could choose to focus my attention on either truth with radically different emotional and behavioral outcomes. It occurred to me that since they were both equally true, it would serve me well to place the focus of my attention on the truth that would give me energy for the moment. Had I not become mindful of this emotional shift, my depressed mood might have of lingered throughout the day. It gave me no energy to be thinking of gardening, but it gave me plenty of energy to be grateful for my work.

By acknowledging that it is possible for two things to be true even though they lead to different actions or that two viewpoints can be true even if they seem opposing, clients are freed from the need to evaluate the two truths and thus can move on to deciding which truth is helpful in the moment.

This chapter has described many strategies to help clients resolve ambivalence by teasing apart various needs to seek the wisdom in both, followed by strategies for reintegrating the various polarities in such a way that resolves the pathological ambivalence. At this point in therapy, clients have learned a lot about the role that pathological ambivalence plays in many of their difficulties, how to understand why there is wisdom in each side, how to harness the ambivalence to understand themselves more fully, and finally how to begin to utilize the wisdom on each side to move forward. Throughout this process, however, it is common for the client to project one part of their ambivalence onto the therapist. The next chapter describes how the therapist can increase skills related to preventing, decreasing, and sidestepping these projections.

Chapter 7: Rewriting False Narratives

When people struggle with pathological ambivalence, it can usually be traced back to a narrative they developed in their past that continues to guide them through life. The scripts in this narrative need to be reevaluated for functionality in the present.

Scripts, Narratives, and Schemas

As discussed throughout this book, people develop scripts, narratives, and schemas as they grow up that help them make sense of the world in which they find themselves. Although these concepts overlap and are sometimes used interchangeably, I think of a *script* as a specific thought, *narratives* as the complex weaving of scripts into a story that guides us through life situations, and *schemas* as the entire set of experiences accompanying the narrative, including thoughts, memories, emotions, and physical sensations.

The brain has formed strong associations among the various components of the schema. If any one of those components is triggered, the entire schema might be experienced. Thus, it is possible to be unaware of parts of the schema when it is operating. For instance, some people feel the sensation of anxiety without realizing that they may have scripts running that are causing it. Other people may be less aware of the physical sensations but obsess on the scripts. It is beneficial, then, to increase awareness of all elements of the schemas for change to occur. Narrative constructivism (Dimaggio, Salatore, Azarra, & Catania, 2003) is a form of therapy that places emphasis on how therapy can be used to rewrite patients' stories through the construction of more adaptive narratives, assisting patients in overcoming their conflicts and tackling the world's complexities.

Identifying Scripts

The first focus for rewriting false narratives is to identify scripts, or the specific beliefs or rules that one has developed about self, others, emotions, and the world. I believe this is the easiest entry point into a person's narrative. I suggest using a structured format for assessing these beliefs like the following example (see also Chapter 5) early in the therapeutic process. Doing this in a structured way reduces shame and misunderstandings because the patient is sharing this information with the therapist, rather than the therapist having to point it out as it occurs or, conversely, completely missing it when it occurs.

Jerry came to therapy for help with an anxiety disorder. He had to travel a great deal for his job, and he obsessed about the weather whenever he had to fly. Several days before each trip, he checked the weather more than 100 times and considered every possible scenario that could possibly go wrong. He had great difficulty sleeping for several days before a flight. Once on the plane, however, he relaxed. During therapy, he revealed that his mother, who could be affectionate, suffered with periodic bouts of depression during his childhood. Jerry was an insightful and sensitive boy, and he tried to monitor his mother's moods to detect subtle changes that might signal an oncoming depression. His father spent a great deal of time with Jerry and was more predictable and stable in mood, but he rarely showed emotion or affection. At 13, his father was tragically killed in a car accident, sending his mother into her longest and deepest depression. Jerry used the Assessment of Beliefs handout found in Appendix A to identify the following beliefs that he had held since childhood:

1. Others are more important than I am.
2. I won't be taken care of.
3. I'm bad, inadequate, guilty.
4. People always leave.
5. Showing emotion is being out of control.
6. The world is dangerous.
7. The world is unpredictable.
8. Life is unfair.
9. The universe is against me.
10. Life is a crap shoot (or a box of chocolates)—you never know what you're going to get.

As is evident, many of Jerry's identified scripts had been projected onto his anxiety about flying. He was totally unaware that these scripts were running and was only aware of his fear of something going wrong (as it often did during his childhood). When asked if the compulsive weather checking reminded him of anything about his childhood, he realized that it did in fact feel similar to watching his mother's face and behaviors for signs that she might be getting depressed. Then with a sheepish expression, he added that the fear that something terrible could happen seemed totally understandable given that his dad had died suddenly. He had come into therapy feeling ashamed and very self-critical about his ridiculous fears; however, his relief was palpable when he first realized that his fears made perfect sense in light of earlier experiences.

Even though this connection was quite obvious to me, rather than interpret it for Jerry, I asked him about it. Remember the rule *never do something for someone that they can do for themselves*. First of all, these connections can seem farfetched when spoken by someone else and second, you could be wrong. When clients interpret for themselves, they are rarely wrong. It was easy for both Jerry and me to see the connection between his early experiences and his fear of being out of control and having bad things unexpectedly happen, as well as a false sense that he could control things that were actually out of his control. He then also began talking about a vague sense of loss and emptiness that he experienced when preparing for a trip, which he had never actually put words to.

As Jerry gained insight into the origin of his schemas, he was able to remind himself that these anxieties were related to his childhood and not to the present concern. This enabled him to begin decreasing the checking behaviors and reducing his overall anxiety.

Scripts Form a Narrative

Jerry was conscious of a script that said "I need to be prepared in case something bad happens," which resulted in the compulsive weather-checking and insomnia. This script then triggered a deeper narrative related to loss of control and a dangerous world about which he was only partially aware. This narrative was in the form of a story that functioned to guide him in life and protect him against possible danger.

Jerry's story formed because he was a sensitive child born into a childhood of much instability. In his story, he had to be hypervigilant to look for cues related to danger. Although he had felt sad and vulnerable, he had interpreted that emotions led to being out of control (like his mother). This narrative in turn triggered an entire schema that encompassed the subconscious experiences of loss and emptiness that occurred periodically when his mother was depressed and traumatically when his father unexpectedly died.

It should be noted that although the relief at these insights was immense, it didn't make the anxiety go away immediately. Jerry still had to go through rewriting his narrative and making behavioral changes through exposure strategies to gradually to overcome the anxieties that had become so habitual over time. He would also have to develop a commitment to rewiring his brain to facilitate a new way of thinking.

False narratives lead to false conclusions. As you can see from Jerry's story, false narratives often result in an interpretation of the world that is limited to one's own early circumstances. These interpretations often lead to global inaccuracies such as the following:

- developing rules about how to live in the world that are incorrect or misguided;
- incorrectly ascribing characteristics to ourselves, such as being unworthy or inadequate;
- making assumptions about others that are inaccurate or premature; and
- believing that we can control people or things over which we actually have no control.

These false conclusions are often the primary reasons that people develop emotional or behavioral disorders which bring them into therapy. For example, someone who believes that she is unworthy of love or attention is likely to develop social anxieties and depression.

Schemas

As described earlier, a schema is a complex group of associated thoughts, beliefs, and physical sensations that are closely associated in the brain and habitually experienced at the same time. Donald Hebb wrote, "The general idea is an old one, that any two cells or systems of cells that are repeatedly active at the same time will tend to become 'associated,' so that activity in one facilitates activity in the other" (1949, p. 70). Further, "When one cell repeatedly assists in firing another, the axon of the first cell develops synaptic knobs (or enlarges them if they already exist) in contact with the soma of the second cell" (p. 63). This phenomenon has been described as "what wires together, fires together."

Thus, a schema can be triggered in the mind if any one of the components is activated. For instance, if a person is under a lot of stress in his daily life that produces anxiety, the anxiety might trigger scripts related to being inadequate. Likewise, if a person gets some constructive feedback on the job, an entire schema might be triggered that involves telling herself that she is not good enough, accompanied by feelings of shame.

It is helpful to educate the client on how a schema operates and how to identify what triggers the schema. In Jerry's situation, he had struggled for years with a vague sense of loss and fear that had expressed itself through his anxiety over flying. Once he identified his scripts and wrote out his previously formed narrative, he was able to address the less conscious aspects of his experiences as well. Subsequently, whenever he felt the sense of loss, he addressed it in a new way by affirming why he was experiencing it and by recognizing that it was related to events of his childhood rather than what was happening in the present moment (also review the concept of idling emotion in Chapter 5). This was a huge improvement over the harsh statements he had made to himself previously.

Similarly, old thoughts and emotions can now be used as a trigger to focus on rewriting the schema. Every time Jerry had an urge to check the weather before a flight, he was encouraged instead to remind himself that it had been very hard to try to predict his mother's depression and that he didn't have to do that anymore. He then followed this with several new scripts that he identified as things he needed to hear and believe.

People develop pathological ambivalence for various reasons, including failure to recognize or accept that they, like everyone else, have basic human needs, while conversely being angry that their needs are not met. Pathological ambivalence is a major obstacle to their growth potential.

Educating clients about basic needs helps them become aware of what they might be denying themselves. There are several lists of needs in the literature, the most famous of which is the Hierarchy of Needs (Maslow, 1943) that has been revised to reflect recent empirical research (Kenrick, Griskevicius, Neuberg, & Schaller, 2010). Maslow proposed that motivation was based on a hierarchy of needs in which some motives have developmental priority over others. The following are the revised needs in ascending order:

- Immediate physiological needs—homeostatic needs essential for survival, such as hunger and thirst
- Self-protection—needs related to safety, dealing with threatening situations, fight-or-flight behaviors
- Affiliation—needs related to belonging to a social group or community
- Status/esteem—needs related to group status and mastery
- Mate acquisition—needs related to love and attracting a mate, which are more likely when status needs are achieved
- Mate retention—needs related to love and stability in relationships
- Parenting (of offspring)—needs related to love and procreation

The format for increasing awareness of basic needs that I find the most helpful was developed by Albert Pesso (1969) in the field of psychomotor therapy. I begin by explaining to my patients that there are universal human needs that every child is born with but not every child gets fully met. In fact, no child gets all their needs met all the time because there are no perfect parents and the world does not present perfect order. Clients are asked to (a) read the basic needs and associated messages; (b) identify the needs that were not fully met due to parental mistakes, early experiences or traumas, or individual level of sensitivity; (c) recognize ways in which they may have been trying subconsciously to get the needs met; and (d) make a plan for getting the needs met in adaptive ways. The basic needs are for nurturance, support, protection, and place. As clients consider exploring the factors related to the development of their story, such as unmet needs, it is natural either to place blame on others who hurt or disappointed them or, in contrast, to resist exploring the story because they don't want to blame anyone else. These are both common reactions. The following is how I explain this to my clients:

If you find yourself getting mad or feeling hurt and you blame someone for his or her actions and their impact on you, you have every right to do so. It may be very important to look directly at how the actions of others have shaped your story, and when doing so, it is natural to feel hurt or angry. However, the primary point of this endeavor is for you to understand all the factors involved so that you can move forward and rewrite your story. Although it goes without saying that people hurt each other, once the pain has been experienced, it becomes the "property," so to speak, of the one who felt it. Thus, your pain is yours to manage and ultimately heal. Many of us wait too long for someone else to heal our pain or change his or her ways. This is a vulnerable endeavor in that we are dependent on someone else to change. I am suggesting that you don't have to wait and that you have the power to change your story independent of anything anyone else does! Although this is great news, some people feel lonely when thinking about letting go of the wish that things had been different or that they have to make the changes on their own without seeing the changes they wish others would make— changes like feeling understood or receiving an apology.

Conversely, if you resist exploring these factors because you fear blaming someone else, then you are not fully dealing with reality. You need to be aware of all the factors that have affected you if you are going to change the way you think.

Increasing Awareness of the Original Story

Using Early Recollections

Early recollections (ERs) is a tool formulated by Alfred Adler (1958), who believed that we selectively remember based on narratives that we form early in life. He developed a strategy for assessing and interpreting early recollections, which can enable a therapist to quickly understand the "lens" through which the patient is viewing the world. The technique is simple: Ask the patient to share the earliest three memories she has as if she were watching it on a video. In reporting the memories, she is to identify the feelings associated with them and the most significant aspect of the memories as if she were to freeze the video at the major point of significance (Kopp & Dinkmeyer, 1975).

Adler also postulated that the ERs could change according to which are remembered or how they are remembered as a result of therapy or other life changes. Some people cannot remember much from before age 10, and thus I devised a research study with the hypothesis that if a person is unable to remember anything before age 10, created ERs might contain the same themes and thus be helpful to the therapeutic process. Subjects were asked to record their earliest memories and then create memories (Buchanan, 1991). These memories were scored and correlated. Results showed that the same themes were present, although the content was at times vastly different in the real versus created memories within individual subjects. This adds further weight to the idea that people are constantly projecting the "Story of My Life" onto all aspects of living. It is the story that needs rewriting for people who are not functioning well.

Writing the False Narrative

It's important that the client become familiar with and conscious of the story he's been telling himself throughout life. Furthermore, it is helpful to understand how the story developed and what factors were involved in its development. I use a template to help people increase awareness of the original problematic narrative. Sometimes, though, people may need to explore any ambivalence they have before doing this. Helpful topics to explore include a fear of blaming others, a desire to hold on to resentment from earlier hurts, wishing someone else would change or apologize, or feeling undeserving of self-care or happiness. When these issues are brought up as common feelings related to changing false narratives, they can be easily addressed. Once the major obstacles to exploring the original story have been addressed, I ask clients to complete a worksheet as an outline for writing out the story that they have been telling themselves. This worksheet (found in

Appendix F, "Template for Writing the False Narrative") includes questions asking about what was challenging during their childhood; what thoughts, beliefs, and rules were developed in response to those challenges; and other factors that may have had an impact on the things that they currently tell themselves.

People are encouraged to explore the most negative or difficult aspects of their childhood first. This is not to focus on the negative but instead has a pragmatic function. In my experience most people unfortunately learn more thoroughly from negative experiences and emotions than from positive ones. Thus, negative experiences—especially for sensitive people with pathological ambivalence—are more readily remembered. In the next section, which focuses on writing a new narrative, clients are instructed to consider the positive experiences as well.

Discrepancies with values. Now the client is prepared to write out the original story. I encourage my clients to write about their original experiences and reactions to these experiences in as much detail as they can. The goal is for them not only to be able to see exactly why they believe and think the way they do, but also to see that the story is no longer working to guide them effectively. It is helpful then to explore discrepancies between the way the story guides them and their current values.

Consider doing a values clarification exercise at this point or, if it has already been done, referring back to it. For instance, Sally indicated that being helpful to others and feeling connected with people was a strong value for her. However, she also had a schema related to remaining invisible because she believed that she was a bad person. Obviously, it's hard for someone who is trying to be invisible to reach out in kindness to another person. When she did act according to her value, her schema was often triggered, and she would say things to herself such as, "She didn't need your help, you shouldn't have done that, or you did it wrong." As she began to understand why she had this urge to hide and be invisible, she gradually could live in line with her values rather than her old story.

Creating a New Narrative

I'm a Person Who ...

To aid in identifying characteristics of the core self, I created a handout called "I'm a Person Who ..." Clients are instructed to read the list and to write an end phrase to each of the sentence stems. I encourage them to go through and do it as quickly as possible without deliberating much on the answer. It is best if they can be open to whatever spontaneous phrase comes to mind without judging how true it may be. The following are a few of the stems:

I'm a person who

_____

I'm a person who likes

_____

I'm a person who loves

_____

I'm a person who wants

_____

I'm a person who gets excited by

_____

I'm a person who doesn't like

_____

I'm a person who is known for

_____

I'm a person who almost never

_____

I'm a person who wishes

_____

I'm a person who admires

_____

I'm a person who gets frustrated when

_____

I'm a person who enjoys

_____

Writing the New Story

Once the client has thoroughly explored the false story and its origins, she is ready to begin writing a new story. As with the old story, I use a similar template to help the client explore what needs to be included in the new story. The template found in Appendix G asks the client to consider what he wished he had known, realized, or understood as a child and how his story may have developed differently if he had known those things. Also included are questions designed to enable the client to consider aspects of his authentic self and his values.

After writing the old story, clarifying values, completing the worksheet for the new story, and filling out the "I'm a Person Who …" worksheet, the client will have done a great deal of research that will enable her to write a new story to replace the original one. This story will focus on aspects of the person that are part of her true and authentic self and include the values that are most important to her. It isn't usually necessary to give much structure to this exercise because it is highly personal and should be a unique creation. The client is simply instructed to write the story that would make sense at this point in her life and may include authentic aspects about her personality, rights, needs, beliefs, and values.

Remember John whose parents divorced when he was 3? After this process, John wrote the following:

> *If I were to tell the story now about that 3-year-old, it would be quite different. I realize now that no 3-year-old has the power to keep parents together who have decided to separate, no matter how loveable he is. I also realize that all children have worth and need stability. As I look back at how hard I tried to earn my parent's love, I see a strength and capacity for commitment that I've never acknowledged. I see that I am a person with a huge capacity for empathy, commitment, and love. I realize that my parents didn't actually leave me, they left each other. They, in fact, both continued to give me messages that I was loved, but those messages were too difficult for me to believe given my assumption about why they separated. I have much to offer people with whom I choose to be in a relationship. I can interact with confidence and expect that most people will see and*

appreciate my genuinely positive characteristics. Some of these people will get to know me well enough to love me and stay.

Strategies for Behavior Change

Although rewriting a new narrative is a powerful change strategy, it is not sufficient by itself to create the lasting change necessary for resolving pathological ambivalence. The brain has been wired to easily trigger the old schemas. Over time, a large amount of "brain real estate" has been devoted to these old patterns. Therefore, it is important to continue working on behavior-change strategies to reinforce the new ways of thinking. Although any effective strategy can be useful, Appendix H includes some that I have found to work best for individuals with pathological ambivalence. These include mindfulness strategies, cognitive-behavioral strategies, and acceptance and commitment therapy (ACT) strategies.

Stand Beside Exercise

Of all the behavior change strategies that I use, the *stand beside exercise* consistently seems to be the most powerful. I developed this experiential exercise based on the ACT concepts of being in the present moment and defusing unhelpful thoughts. I ask the participant to consider a thought that often occurs from the old schema such as "People will reject me." I then guide them through the following instructions.

1. Stand up and begin thinking the thought and noticing whatever else is part of the schema.
2. Label the emotions and notice any physical sensations.
3. Notice what this thought makes you want to do.
4. Take a step aside as if you can step back and look at the thought.
5. Consider the history of the thought and any distortions.
6. What would you like, now, to say to that thought from your new narrative?
7. What would it feel like to turn your back to the thought?
8. Can you now walk away from the thought?

Sometimes I suggest that the person step back into the spot where he first stood to connect with the thought again and then repeat the process of stepping aside for further practice of thought diffusion. I've also used this exercise in a group setting, adding the instruction that each person notice that the person next to them just "stepped into your thought." I ask them to notice what they think about the other person having to think his or her thought and if they have any advice to offer about it. They are often much more able to connect with their wisdom about the thought when they look at it through someone else's eyes.

Summary

In this chapter, I have described how scripts are formed and how they weave together to form narratives, which then become wired into the brain in the form of complex schemas. I've discussed the importance of helping your clients increase awareness of all these components and offered strategies for doing this. These include learning to identify scripts through mindful awareness, use of early recollections, embracing the concept of universal needs, and writing the old narrative. The next task, then, is to help them reevaluate the old story by increasing awareness of their identity and values and then weaving these insights into a new narrative. Thus, regardless of how pathological a person's ambivalence may be, the story behind it can be rewritten and the brain rewired.

Epilogue: Concluding Thoughts

It is my hope that after reading this book, you will have developed a mind-set and gained a set of strategies that enable you to feel competent with your clients who present as resistant. I hope that, rather than feeling confused, you will be curious about the journey you and your clients share and explore the interacting neurological, psychological, and situational mechanisms that lead to ambivalence. My theory of pathological ambivalence encompasses why people experience ambivalence, the factors that make some people more susceptible than others to developing pathological ambivalence, and how inaccurate narratives are formed that create problems for them in life.

Without a theoretical understanding of pathological ambivalence and a roadmap for using strategies for change, you might feel confused by your clients' fear of change. They come to you asking for help, but they don't do the things that you suggest—and may even blame you for their lack of change. Their fear about change is often characterized as resistant, oppositional, or unmotivated. However, because they fear the very thing that they are asking you to help them do, this must be addressed directly. It is my hope that these concepts allow you to disentangle from the various ways that clients present ambivalence so that you don't find yourself at odds with them.

My goal is that, rather than getting stuck on one side of the ambivalence, you have learned specific ways to help your clients first to see the dialectics in their experience by increasing their own awareness of their disparate thoughts and feelings and then to help them harness and integrate these thoughts and feelings to build the life they desire. Rather than therapy being slowed by ambivalence, these strategies actually enable the ambivalence to be harnessed in a way that speeds up the therapeutic process by getting to the heart of the matter in the earliest sessions.

In this book, I have introduced the concept of pathological ambivalence from a variety of theoretical perspectives. This is because there is no one theory that encompasses all concepts involved or that fits for every client. I hope this has enabled you to integrate all of your education and experience with the concepts and strategies described here. I encourage you to experiment and adapt these techniques, and others that you find useful, to your own style and practice. Make it your own so that it fits your unique and authentic self as a clinician. I believe that patients feel comforted when they sense that we are being ourselves.

I attempted to bring the strategies to life by incorporating stories about the courageous people with whom I have worked over the years. Most of what I've learned about treating ambivalence, I've learned from them. I encourage you to be fascinated with your ambivalent clients and respect any strengths that you see, even when they seem to be interfering with treatment. Conceptualizing clients as ambivalent will enable you to embrace the specific challenges and deep rewards that can occur in your work with them.

Appendix A: Worksheets for Assessment

Assessment of Beliefs

The following are samples of previously held beliefs that you may have formed throughout life that are no longer helpful. These samples provide a jumping-off point to help with brainstorming, but feel free to rewrite them in your own words or add to the list.

Beliefs About Self:

_____Others are more important than I am.

_____I don't make sense.

_____I'm important only because of what I can accomplish.

_____I'll sound foolish.

_____I'm not likeable.

_____I won't be taken care of.

_____I'm too much.

_____I'm bad, inadequate, guilty.

Beliefs About Others:

_____People will judge me.

_____People will be critical.

_____People care only about themselves.

_____People can't be trusted.

_____People won't understand.

_____People always leave.

Beliefs About Emotions:

_____Don't show anger—it's bad.

_____Don't let people see you cry—they'll think you're weak.

_____Negative emotions are wrong.

_____Showing emotion is being out of control.

_____There is a right way to feel about things.

Beliefs About the World:
____The world is dangerous.
____The world is unpredictable.
____Life is unfair.
____The universe is against me.
____Life is a crap shot (or box of chocolates)—you never know what you're going to get.
____Other

The beliefs that you checked off lead to specific behaviors. Complete the following sentence to increase insight into how each of your beliefs is currently operating in your life.

I have a need for _____, which I use my symptom to meet because I have not yet been able to believe_____. I continue this way even though it makes me_____.

Window of Opportunity Journaling Handout

Sometimes it is difficult to know how problematic behaviors are functioning without further increasing your insight. I created this form of journaling to specifically increase awareness. People journal in many ways and for different reasons (i.e., getting out their feelings or keeping a diary of their life experiences). This is a very specific form of journaling with a very specific function. Important information about yourself is available to you as an urge rises to use a symptom or behave in an ineffective way (e.g., avoiding, yelling, binging, drinking). The urge rises for particular reasons, and if you can pause for a few moments while the urge is high and increase your self-awareness, you will begin to understand yourself more fully. It is as if there is a window of opportunity that is wide open when your urge is high, but that window slams shut once one engages in the problematic behavior. This happens because the behavior functions quite effectively, although only temporarily, to relieve the urge.

Clients often identify with this when you ask if they engage in a problematic behavior and later in a counseling session can't fully explain why things seemed so bad at the time. I explain that in those moments, important information such as their insecurities, perceived unmet needs, and old hurts are present in their experience, leading to a need to engage in the problematic behavior. Possibly everything they need to know to understand why they are struggling is captured in the feelings at those moments. However, after using the behavior, the thoughts, beliefs, and feelings go underground again, so to speak, because the window is no longer open. I suggest that if they can write down some of what they are feeling in the moment and then take it into their next session to talk over with the therapist, they will get more bang for their buck.

Clients can be instructed as follows: You can use these questions to facilitate the experience of pausing at this time to understand yourself and your symptoms more fully. The questions are a starting point and that you are free to write about anything that comes to mind. I suggest an optimal time of 15 minutes (some set a timer) after which if you still want to engage in the symptom or behavior (with the exception of behaviors that hurt others or are suicidal in nature), you can still consider the endeavor a success because simply by journaling, you have taken an important step in increasing your self-awareness. The following questions are just a suggested starting point; feel free to ask yourself other questions as well.

1. What am I feeling right now (in feeling words such as *anger, hurt,* etc.)?
2. What changes am I aware of in my body (stomach, jaw, shoulders, etc.) as I'm feeling this emotion?
3. What happened to make me feel this way?
4. Is this a familiar feeling in that it comes up often?
5. Could this feeling be related to ways I felt as a child? If so how?
6. When was the first time I ever felt this way, and what was happening at that time?
7. What did I need then but didn't get?
8. How would engaging in _____ help with this feeling?
9. How would I feel immediately after engaging in _____?
10. How would I feel later?
11. What would happen if I didn't engage in _____?
12. When someone is feeling this way, what does he or she truly need?
13. What do I need from myself when I am feeling this way?
14. Is there anything I can do other than engaging in _____ that would help even a little?

As stated earlier, 15 minutes is a goal, and I can almost guarantee that if you work on this for 15 minutes at the critical moment, something important will happen. However, when urges are particularly strong, many people can't start at this level. Therefore, it's okay to start as small as you need to. For instance, the first step may simply be buying the journal and placing it in a strategic location. Next, you might only have the ability to open and write one word, preferably a feeling word. A fun variation on this is to have a box of crayons near the journal, and you can choose a color to match the emotion. Next time, you might write just one phrase, then a sentence, and then write for five minutes and so on. It is important that small successes are celebrated. Additionally, some people are averse to writing, so we might explore other avenues, such as dictating into a phone or sketching an image representing what's going on, for example. Although I'm accepting of any starting point, I generally do tell people that there is something powerful about handwriting in that it slows the brain and communicates to ourselves that we are worth the time and effort. Finally, if you are unable to pause in the moment, I suggest you use the handout that as soon as possible after engaging in the behavior.

Appendix B: Treatment Plans and Contracts

Client-Centered Treatment Planning

In Chapter 5, you learned about assessing clients' beliefs, their dysfunctional behaviors, how their symptoms are functioning, and their level motivation. After a thorough assessment has been conducted, treatment planning can ensue. It is important to develop specific behavioral goals that are mutually agreed on between the therapist and client. Goal-setting will be driven by the factors that brought the person into therapy and needs to be described as concretely as possible. The three general categories for goal setting in the treatment plan can be conceptualized as follows: (1) harnessing and moving through ambivalence about making the changes, (2) decreasing dysfunctional behaviors, and (3) increasing functional thoughts and behaviors.

With pathological ambivalence, working through the ambivalence is the meat of the therapy. The goals in the second and third categories may be met naturally during the process of working through the ambivalence. Nevertheless, it is important to discuss what specific changes you and the patient hope to see occur during this process.

Initial Contracts

Initial contracts with all patients focus on the parameters of your practice (such as billing, scope, hours available, etc.) and the treatment plan. For patients with pathological ambivalence, the initial contracts may also need to include a section on what Marsha Linehan refers to as *therapy-interfering behaviors*, including missing appointments, coming late to sessions, drinking or using other addictive behaviors, and even entertaining thoughts or making threats of suicide. It is important to address these potential therapy-interfering behaviors early in the process, so that the client is prepared to deal with them as she is contemplating change and to view them as a common sign of change rather than a reason to back away.

Sample Goal Section of a Treatment Plan

1. Harnessing and moving through ambivalence

   Understanding the obstacles to change
   Recognizing beliefs or narratives that make change difficult
   Honoring the wisdom on both sides of the ambivalence

2. Decreasing dysfunctional behaviors

   Social withdrawal
   Reluctance to express opinions and feelings

3. Increasing functional thoughts and feelings

   Initiate social interactions
   Develop belief in own worth
   Develop skills for dealing with anxiety
   Increase self-confidence

Appendix C: The Shame–Humility–Guilt–Regret Continuum

	Toxic Shame	Natural Humility	Guilt	Regret/ Sadness
Thoughts are Characterized by	Identity thought "I" statements: I am bad I am unworthy I am inadequate I am unacceptable	I am human I am flawed but wonderful I am connected to other imperfect human beings It could have happened to anyone I make mistakes like everyone else	I have done something wrong I have done something that I wish I didn't do	I did something wrong, but there is nothing else to learn or do about it I understand why and have compassion for the mistake I made and will always feel a little sad or regretful when it comes to mind
Preceeding Event	An unspecified action I feel responsible for someone else's action.	A specific action or behavior I did something embarassing or humbling	A specific action or behavior in the recent past	A specific action in the recent or further past

Duration of Emotion	Long term Pervasive Overwhelming	Short term	Short term if corrected Pervasive until corrective action taken	Long term Not pervasive
Action Urge	Hide Disappear	Momentary urge to hide Laugh at humanness	Apologize for wrongdoing Learn from mistake	None

When dealing with one of these feelings, ask yourself the following questions to help you identify the correct emotion and determine a course of action:

1. What has made me feel this way?
2. Is this feeling motivating me to do anything productive?
3. Is this feeling making me feel that "*I am*" bad, inadequate, unlovable, etc.?
4. Did I do something wrong, but I have already done everything I can do to correct it?
5. Am I feeling bad because of something someone else did?
6. What is this feeling making me want to do?
7. Is what I did something that anyone may have done and feel embarrassed about?
8. Is my feeling specific to a particular incident, or does it feel pervasive?

Appendix D: Additional Strategies for Challenging Status Quo

Examining the Pros and Cons

A well-established format for working through ambivalence focuses on identifying the pros and cons of a course of action. This endeavor is often called a cost–benefit analysis or split column journaling. For example, exploring the reasons for and against stopping smoking might look something like this:

Cost–Benefit Analysis for Stopping Smoking

Pros	Cons
• Improve lung health • Improve heart health • Eat in more restaurants • Won't smell like smoke • Please my husband • Won't have to hide my smoking from my kids	• Will be physically difficult due to addiction to nicotine • It is pleasurable • Helps me relax • Gives me a break

This exercise enables the person to see why she has said for years that she wants to stop smoking but still haven't been successful.

Examining Exceptions to the Problem

Solution-focused brief therapy (SFBT) was developed by Steve de Shazer and Insoo Kim Berg and their colleagues beginning in the late 1970s in Milwaukee, WI. The entire solution-focused approach was developed inductively rather than theory driven as the developers spent hundreds of hours observing therapy sessions over the course of several years, carefully noting the therapists' questions and activities that affected the clients and the therapeutic outcome of the sessions. Questions and activities related to clients' report of progress were incorporated into the SFBT approach. All the tools of SFBT are aimed at helping the client form his or her own vision of solutions.

One such strategy is asking the client to talk about exceptions to his problem or times when the problem is not occurring or is less significant (de Shazer, 1982). He is then asked to focus on what is happening instead at these times. This is another strategy for highlighting that there are two sides to clients' stories. For example, Tina said that she always felt depressed and that she didn't think she was ever going to feel better. She could not even picture a future without depression. When asked to talk about times when her depression was even a little better, she mentioned being with her niece and described the experience as one of being very content and feeling special. The problem was that because of her depression, she felt that she didn't have the energy to go to her sister's house to spend time with her niece. Rather than focusing on her depression, we focused on getting her together with her niece.

Miracle Question

Another SFBT strategy is called the Miracle Question (Berg & Dolan, 2001). The client is asked something like this:

> Let's say that while you are sleeping tonight, a miracle occurs: When you awake tomorrow morning, your problem will be completely solved, and your day will unfold as it would if the problem were completely resolved. What is the first thing that you would notice is different, and how would your day be different than it is now?

This exercise can facilitate several helpful things, but in regard to creating an imbalance in the status quo, it helps the client look through a positive lens into her hopes and wishes rather than focusing on how difficult it is to change

Jenny struggled with emotional overeating. She alternated between restricting and overeating and was plagued with constant preoccupation with thoughts of food. She was trapped in a cycle in which she would attempt to restrict throughout the day but become so hungry that she would overeat in the evenings. When asked the miracle question, she talked about getting up in the morning and having a nourishing breakfast. She described being interested in the events of the day and having balance in work and play. She would never skip lunch and would make sure that she ate in balance throughout the day. Jenny imagined that she would have more energy to do the things that she enjoyed. After work, she would go to her photography class, something that she had talked about doing for years but never had. She said she would be looking forward to a party that she was going to that weekend because since she was feeling more comfortable in her body, she would be accepting social invitations.

The miracle question can then be followed by asking what parts of this miracle day are already happening or could begin happening immediately. Jenny responded that she could sign up for a photography class and made that an immediate goal.

Gestalt Body Work

Posture, movements of hands and feet, facial expression, and voice intonation may convey feelings that the client is unaware of or unable to express verbally (Stephenson, 1978). The function of the therapist is to redirect the patient's attention to his own experience by asking questions such as the following:

"Are you aware of what you are doing with your hands?"

"I noticed your voice sounds different now; can you hear it?"

I was once sitting next to a patient in a group setting, and our chairs were touching. She was bouncing her leg so hard that it was bouncing me in my seat. I asked her, "Patty, what is your leg trying to say right now?" After pausing for a few moments, she answered that she thought of something to say in group but had no right to do so. I pointed out that her leg felt differently and definitely wanted to express something. She was then able to discuss her ambivalence about talking, which was much better than honoring only the part of her that said to be quiet. In this example, her bouncing leg was honoring the part of her that wanted to speak.

Appendix E: Additional Strategies for Integrating Splits

Split-Column Journaling

With split-column journaling, the client is instructed to draw a vertical line down the middle of the page. The two columns are then labeled according to the topic of ambivalence, such as "quit job" and "stay with job." Then all thoughts about the topic are written in one of the columns depending on which side of the dilemma it falls.

After all related thoughts are written down, the person sits back and looks at the two sides, thus using wise mind and prefrontal lobes. The client is then instructed to highlight the wisdom on either side with one color and highlight the fallacies on either side with another color. Even choosing a color is a mindful approach to integration. Finally, the client is asked to imagine that she is the wisest person in the world and will now begin to decide which thoughts to discard, which thoughts to validate, and which thoughts to reassure in a new way. This endeavor creates an integration of both sides that will almost always point to the direction for change. It is important to pay close attention to the thoughts the client has decided to discard, as these are usually fueled by anxiety related to early narratives. The client will need to be specific with herself about how to take care of the embedded anxiety in new ways, such as reminding herself that she has many friends now who find her lovable, even though she has trouble always believing it due to old scripts.

Self-Portraits or Photos

Another technique for increasing awareness for the purpose of integration is using pictures. A client can be encouraged to find pictures of himself at the ages that seem to be represented by the ambivalence. If the child part feels about 6 years old, then the client can put pictures of himself at this age in his environment (a form of environmental manipulation) to remind him to pay attention to this part during the day. This prompts him to think *about* this part of himself rather than be experiencing the moment only from the child part. Similarly, if the adolescent part feels 13, then pictures of himself at this age will also be placed in his environment. In this way, he can increase awareness of whenever he is telling himself old rules or when old schemas are operating. Additionally, the very act of finding pictures and developing a nurturing, kind attitude toward oneself in the pictures can be life changing for people who have struggled with shame throughout their lives.

For artistic clients, the therapist might suggest that they create self-portraits of their child and adolescent ego state, using whatever medium they prefer. These then can be placed in their environment to prompt mindful awareness and the activation of the adult ego state.

Guided Imagery

Guided imagery works in a similar manner to letters to self. The client is guided to imagine herself at the age she began to develop beliefs about herself that are now proving dysfunctional. She can then be guided to imagine that her wise self is sitting with her younger self and having a conversation.

Appendix F: Template for Writing the False Narrative

The most difficult aspects of my childhood were (list as many as you can think of)

_____

_____

The feelings that I experienced because of this were

_____

I adjusted to these feelings by:

Thoughts_____

_____

Beliefs_____

_____

Rules_____

_____

Behaviors_____

_____

Additional factors that may have played a part in the formation of my story:

Individual factors (highly sensitive personality, physical factors, attention-deficit/hyperactivity disorder, birth order, etc.)_____

_____

Situational factors (family structure, parental mistakes, traumatic experiences such as death, divorce, moving, etc.)_____

_____

Appendix G: Template for Writing the New Narrative

What I wish I'd known as a child_____

What I wish someone had explained to me_____

What I wish I could have believed at the
time_____

If I'd known and believed these things the following might be different:

Thoughts_____
_____

Beliefs_____
_____

Rules_____
_____

Behaviors_____
_____

The strengths and positive qualities that I demonstrated in childhood
are _____

Things that I have gained through my early hurtful experiences
_____

The most positive aspects of my childhood were
_____

The feelings that I experienced due to this were
_____

Had I known what I know now, these experiences might have affected me by:

Thoughts_____

_____

Beliefs_____

_____

Behaviors_____

_____

Characteristics of my authentic self

_____

Values that I most want to incorporate into my new
story_____

Appendix H: Strategies for Creating Behavioral Change

Mindfulness Strategies

All strategies that teach people to pause, observe their internal processes, and choose how to respond in the moment rather than react will enable them to notice when the old schema is being triggered and to focus instead on the new narrative. The Distress Tolerance and Emotion Management strategies of dialectical and behavioral therapy (Linehan, 1993) are especially helpful in this endeavor.

Acceptance and Commitment Therapy (ACT)

The general goal of ACT is to increase psychological flexibility—the ability to contact the present moment more fully as a conscious human being, and to change or persist in behavior when doing so to live consistently with values. Psychological flexibility is established through six core ACT processes. Each of these areas is conceptualized as a positive psychological skill, not merely a method of avoiding psychopathology (see the Association for Contextual and Behavioral Science website submitted by Steven Hayes: https://contextualscience.org/aboutact). The six processes are Acceptance, Cognitive Fusion, Being Present, Self as Context, Values, and Committed. Although it is beyond the scope of this book to fully describe these processes and the multiple strategies that have been devised to encourage them, the reader is referred to the website as a wonderful resource in building skills in these areas.

Particularly relevant to creating behavior change after the development of a new narrative is the concept of cognitive fusion. Due to brain physiology, the old story is, in a sense, fused with the self. Although it may take years for the old thoughts to fade, the following techniques are useful in diffusing thought from self in the current moment.

Computer Virus Metaphor

I heard a story about a computer virus that may or may not be true, but it is a great metaphor for how we can diffuse our thoughts. Apparently, if the virus attacked your computer, the screen would go blank, and then words to the effect of "you are a big idiot" would appear. The only thing that would make the virus go away was to type OK. I can imagine that it was frustrating to hit OK in response to this statement. However, if you did, your computer would return to normal.

Similarly if an old negative thought were to pop up in your mind, especially one that is difficult to refute such as "You should have done better," it would be very effective to simply say okay and move on to the next thought. This would neutralize the thought.

Opening Space Around the Experience

This concept is based on accepting what is but opening space around it to decrease avoidance of what is and to see what else might also be true. In this endeavor, a client can be taught to accept that he believes people will be rejecting and that it might take a long time to change this belief. Rather than fight what is, one accepts the pain and then breathes some space around it. The client can learn that it isn't necessary to wait until the thoughts and feelings have changed to begin to live differently. This can be done in a breathing exercise with visualization.

Control Knobs

A well-known metaphor (Hayes, Strosahl, & Wilson, 1999, pp. 133–134) asks the person to think of two control knobs, one that sets the amount of emotional distress (e.g., anxiety high or low) and one that sets the degree of willingness to have that distress. When anxiety is high and willingness is low, anxiety becomes something to be anxious about—it self-amplifies. A client can be taught that increasing the willingness to feel the anxiety actually diffuses the anxiety and offers an increased opportunity to experience other aspects of the situation.

Cognitive Strategies

Hypothesis Testing

Hypothesis-testing strategies (Arkowitz et al., 1989) involve the client in actively seeking and questioning the evidence that supports their particular beliefs and checking the probabilities that what they fear, as a result of their beliefs, will occur. The client will be asked questions such as, "How likely do you think this is?" and "What is the likely outcome?" Appraisals of high probability and very bad outcomes lead to anxiety and avoidance. Clients are taught to search for evidence that gives them an accurate appraisal of the likelihood that the problem will occur as a basis for changing their thoughts and thus their behavior. It is easy to see how this fits into the concept that an individual's narratives or scripts can be rewritten.

Identifying Distortions

In David Burns classic book *Feeling Good: The New Mood Therapy*, first published in 1980 (newest edition, 2008), he identified 10 cognitive distortions that can be taught to clients to help them see patterns in the ways that they evaluate experiences. These include *all-or-nothing thinking, overgeneralization, catastrophizing, "should" statements, personalization, and blame.* Once clients have identified a pattern, they can raise awareness of these distortions as they arise and learn to challenge the thought, resulting in behavior change.

References

Adler, A. (1964). *Individual psychology of Alfred Adler.* New York, NY: HarperCollins.

Adler, A. (2014). Understanding human nature. New York, NY: Routledge. (Original work published 1928)

Acevedo, B. P., Aron, E. N., Aron, A., Snagster, M. D., Collins, N., & Brown, L. L. (2014). The highly sensitive brain: An fMRI study of sensory processing sensitivity and response to others' emotions. Brain and Behavior, 4, 580–594.

American Heritage Dictionary. (2011a). Ambivalence. Retrieved from https://ahdictionary.com/word/search.html?q=ambivalence

American Heritage Dictionary. (2011b). Pathology. Retrieved from https://ahdictionary.com/word/search.html?q=pathology

American Psychiatric Association. (1994). Diagnostic and statistical manual of mental disorders (4th ed.). Washington, DC: Author.

Anderman, E. M., & Anderman, L. H. (2009). Psychology of classroom learning: An encyclopedia. Detroit, MI: Macmillan Reference USA/Gale Cengage Learning.

Anderson, C. M., & Stewart, S. (1983). Mastering resistance: A practical guide to family therapy. New York, NY: Guilford Press.

Arcelus J., Mitchell, A. J., Wales, J., & Nielsen, S. (2011). Mortality rates in patients with anorexia nervosa and other eating disorders. Archives of General Psychiatry, 68, 724–731.

Arkowitz, H., Beutler, L. E., & Simon, K. (1989). Cognitive handbook of cognitive therapy. New York, NY: Plenum Press.

Aron, E. (1996). The highly sensitive person. New York, NY: Kensington.

Bacon, F. (2000). The new organon. Cambridge, England: Cambridge University Press. Original work published 1620

Banks, S. J., Kamryn, T. E., Angstadt, M., Pradeep, N. J. & Phan, L. K. (2007). Amygdala–frontal connectivity during emotion regulation. Social Cognitive and Affective Neuroscience, 2, 303–3120.

Berg, I. K., & Dolan, Y. (2001). Tales of solutions: A collection of hope-inspiring stories. New York, NY: Norton.

Berne, E. (1961). Transactional analysis in psychotherapy. New York, NY: Grove Press.

Bradshaw, J. (1988). Healing the shame that binds you. Deerfield Beach, FL: Health Communications.

Buchanan, L. P., Kern, R., & Bell-Dumas, J. (1991, September). A comparison of created versus actual early recollections. Individual Psychology, 348–355.

Burns, D. (2008). Feeling good: The new mood therapy. New York, NY: HarperCollins.

Cahill, L., & McGaugh, J. L. (1995). A novel demonstration of enhanced memory associated with emotional arousal. Consciousness and Cognition, 4, 410–421.

Carkhuff, R. R. (1972). The art of helping. Amherst, MA: HRD Press.

Caspi, A., Hariri, A. R., Holmes, A., Uher, R., & Moffitt, T. E. (2010). Genetic sensitivity to the environment: The case of the serotonin transporter gene (5-HTT) and its implications for studying complex diseases and traits. American Journal of Psychiatry, 167, 509–527.

De Bellis, M. D. (2001). Developmental traumatology: The psychobiological development of maltreated children and its implications for research, treatment, and policy. Developmental Psychopathology, 13, 539–564.

De Bellis, M. D., & Zisk, A. B. (2014). The biological effects of childhood trauma. Child and Adolescent Psychiatry Clinics, 23, 185–222.

DeRubeis R. J, Siegle G. J., & Hollon S. D. (2008). Cognitive therapy versus medication for depression: treatment outcomes and neural mechanisms. National Review Neuroscience, 9, 788–796.

de Shazer, S. (1982). Patterns of brief family therapy. An ecosystemic approach. New York, NY: Guilford Press.

Dimaggio, G., Salatore, G., Azzara, C., & Catania, D. (2003). Rewriting self-narratives: Therapeutic process. Journal of Constructivist Psychology, 16, 155–181.

Engle, D. E., & Arkowitz, H. (2006). Ambivalence in psychotherapy: Facilitating readiness to change. New York, NY: Guilford Press.

Erickson, M. H., Rossi, E. L., & Rossi, S. I. (1976). Hypnotic realities: The induction of clinical induction and forms of indirect suggestion. New York, NY: Irvington.

Fox, E., Zouqkou, K., Ridgewell, A., & Garner, K. (2011). The serotonin transporter gene alters sensitivity to attention bias modification: Evidence for a plasticity gene. Biological Psychiatry, 70, 1049–1054.

Frankl, V. (2006). Man's search for meaning. Boston, MA: Beacon Press. (Original work published 1946)

Freud, S. (1959a). Psychopathology. In J. Strachey, A. Freud, & C. L. Rothgeb (Eds.), The standard edition of the complete psychological works of Sigmund Freud: Vol. 13. London: Hogarth Press; New York, NY: Macmillan.

Freud, S. (1959b). Inhibitions, symptoms and anxiety. In J. Strachey, A. Freud, & C. L. Rothgeb (Eds.), standard edition of the complete psychological works of Sigmund Freud: Vol. 20 (pp. 77–178). London: Hogarth Press; New York: Macmillan.

Freud, S. (1959c). Further recommendations in the technique of psychoanalysis: Recollection, repetition, and working through. In E. Jones & J. Riviere (Eds. and Trans.), Collected Papers (Vol. 2, pp. 366–376). New York, NY: Basic Books.

Griffith, J., & Powers, R. L. (2007). The lexicon of Adlerian psychology: 106 terms associated with the individual psychology of Alfred Adler (2nd ed.). Chicago, IL: Adlerian Psychology Associates.

Hanson, R. (2011). Just one thing: Developing a Buddha brain one simple practice at a time. Oakland, CA: New Harbinger.

Harris, T. A. (1967). I'm okay, you're okay. New York, NY: Harper.

Hayes, S. C. (n.d.). About ACT as found at https://contextualscience.org/about_act

Hayes, S. C., Strosahl, K., & Wilson, K. G. (1999). Acceptance and commitment therapy: An experiential approach to behavior change. New York, NY: Guilford Press.

Hebb, D. O. (1949). The organization of behavior: A neuropsychological theory. New York, NY: Wiley.

Hegel, G. W. F. (1952). The philosophy of right. (Trans. T.M. Knox). In R. M. Hutchins & M .J. (Eds.), Great books of the western world, Volume 46. Adler. Chicago, IL

Hendrix, H. (2005). Getting the love you want (reissue ed.). New York, NY: Perennial.

Karg, K., Burmeister, M., Shedden, K., & Sen, S. (2011). The serotonin transporter promoter variant (5-HTTLPR), stress, and depression meta-analysis revisited: Evidence of genetic moderation. Archives of General Psychiatry, 68, 444–454.

Kendler, K. S., & Prescott, C. A. (2006). Genes, environment, and psychopathology. New York, NY: Guilford Press.

Kenrick, D. T., Griskevicius, V., Neuberg, S. L., & Schaller, M. (2010). Renovating the pyramid of needs: Contemporary extensions built upon ancient foundations. Perspectives on Psychological Science, 5, 292–314.

Kernberg, O. F. (1985). Internal world and external reality: Object relations theory applied. Lanham, MD: Aronson.

Kishor, V. (2015). Inspiring thoughts of great educational thinkers. Naharashtra, India: Amitesh.

Kopp, R. R., & Dinkmeyer, D. (1975). Early recollections in life style assessment and counseling. The School Counselor, 23(1), 22–27.

Krystal, A. D. (2006). Sleep and psychiatric disorders: Future directions. Psychiatric Clinics of North America, 29, 1115–1130.

Latner, J. (2000). The theory of gestalt therapy. In E. Nevis (Ed.), Gestalt therapy: Perspectives and applications. Cambridge, MA: Gestalt Press.

Lazarus, A.A. & Fay, A. (1982). Resistance or rationalization? A cognitive-behavioral perspective. In P. L. Wachtel (Ed.), Resistance: Psychodynamic and behavioral approaches (pp. 115–132). New York, NY: Plenum Press.

Leahy, R. L. (2003). Overcoming resistance in cognitive therapy. New York, NY: Guilford Press.

LeBlanc, A. (2001). The origins of the concept of dissociation: Paul Janet, his nephew Pierre, and the problem of post-hypnotic suggestion, History of Science, 39, 57–69.

Linehan, M. M. (1993). Cognitive-behavioral treatment of borderline personality disorder. New York, NY: Guilford Press.

Liu, D. L., Graham, S., & Zorawaski, M. (2008). Enhanced selective memory consolidation following post-learning pleasant and aversive arousal. Neurobiology of Learning and Memory, 89, 36–46.

Lyttle, N., Dorahy M. J., Hanna, D., & Huntjens, R. J. (2010). Conceptual and perceptual priming and dissociation in chronic posttraumatic stress disorder. Journal of Abnormal Psychology, 119, 777–790.

Madanes, C. (1981). Strategic family therapy. San Francisco, CA: Jossey-Bass.

Mahler, M. S., Pine, F., & Bergman, A. (1975). The psychological birth of the human infant: Symbiosis and individuation. New York, NY: Basic Books.

Marcus, P., & Rosenberg, A. (Eds.). (1998). Psychoanalytic versions of the human condition: Philosophies of life and their impact on practice. New York, NY: NYU Press.

Maslow, A. H. (1943). A theory of human motivation. Psychological Review, 50, 370–396.

Mateer, C., & Kerns, K. (2000). Capitalizing on neuroplasticity. Brain and Cognition, 42, 106–109.

McDonald, J., & Carroll, J. (1992). Communication with young children: An ecological model for clinicians, parents and collaborative professionals. American Journal of Speech-Language Pathology, 1(4), 39–48.

McGaugh, J. L. (2000). Memory-a century of consolidation. Science, 287, 248–251.

Messer, S. B. (2002). A psychodynamic perspective on resistance in psychotherapy: Vive la résistance. Journal of Clinical Psychology, 58, 157–163.

Merzinich, M. (2013). Soft-wired: How the new science of brain plasticity can change your life (2nd ed.). San Francisco, CA: Parnassus.

Michael, T., Ehlers, A., & Halligan, S.L. (2005). Enhanced priming for trauma-related material in posttraumatic stress disorder. Emotion, 5, 103–112.

Miller, A. (1981). Drama of the gifted child. Boston, MA: Basic Books.

Minuchin, S. (1974). Families and family therapy. London, England: Tavistock.

Minuchin, S., & Fishman, H. C. (2004). Family therapy techniques. Cambridge, MA: Harvard University Press.

Mitchell, C. W. (2012). Effective methods for dealing with highly resistant clients (4th ed.). Johnson City, TN: Clifton Mitchell.

Morgan, A. (2000). What is narrative therapy? An easy-to-read introduction. London, England: Dulwich Centre.

Mozak, H. E. (1958). Early recollections as a projective technique. Journal of Projective Techniques, 22, 302–311.

Mosak, H. H. (1985). Interrupting a depression: The pushbutton technique. Individual Psychology: Journal of Adlerian Theory, Research & Practice, 41, 210–214.

Mushtaq, A. M., & Mushtaq, D. (2011). Serotonin transporter gene polymorphism and psychiatric disorders: Is there a link? Indian Journal of Psychiatry, 53, 288–299.

Nichols, M. P., & Schwartz, R. C. (2012). Family therapy concepts and methods. New York, NY: Pearson.

Norwood, R. (1985). Women who love too much. New York, NY: Pocket Books.

Ni, X. Q., Chan K., Bulgin, N., Sicard T., Bismil R., McMain S., & Kennedy, J. L. (2007). Association between serotonin transporter gene and borderline personality disorder. Journal of Psychiatric Research, 40, 448–453.

Ni, X., Chan, D., Chan, K., McMain, S., & Kennedy, J.L. (2009). Serotonin genes and gene–gene interactions in borderline personality disorder in a matched case–control study. Progressive Neuropsychopharmacological Biological Psychiatry, 33, 128–133.

Perls, F. S., Hefferline, R., & Goodman, P. (1977). Gestalt therapy: Excitement and growth in the human personality. Gouldsboro, ME: The Gestalt Journal Press. (Original work published 1951)

Pesso, A. (1969). Movement in psychotherapy: Psychomotor techniques and training. New York, NY: New York University Press.

Piaget, J. (1954). The construction of reality in the child. New York, NY: Basic Books.

Piaget, J. (1964). The early growth of logic in the child. London, England: Routledge and Kegan Paul.

Piaget, J. (1972). The principles of genetic epistemology. New York, NY: Basic Books.

Paquette, V., Levesque, J., Mensour, B., Jean-Maximel, L., Beaudoin, G., Bourgouin, P., & Bearuegard, M. (2003). Change the mind and you change the brain: Effects of cognitive-behavioral therapy on the neural correlates of spider phobia. NeuroImage, 18, 401–409.

Polster, E., & Polster, M. (1973). Gestalt therapy integrated: Contours of theory and practice. New York, NY: Brunner-Mazel

Prochaska, J. O., Norcross, J. C., & DiClemente, C. C. (1994). Changing for good: The revolutionary program that explains the six stages of change and teaches you how to free yourself from bad habits. New York, NY: Morrow.

Reichborn-Kjennerud, T. (2010). The genetic epidemiology of personality disorders. Dialogues in Clinical Neuroscience, 12, 103–114.

Ribeiro, P. A., Goncalves, M. M., Siva, J. R., Bras, A., & Sousa, I. (2016). Ambivalence in narrative therapy: A comparison between recovered and unchanged cases. Clinical Psychology and Psychotherapy, 23, 166–174.

Rozin, P., & Royzman, E. B. (2001). Negativity bias, negativity dominance, and contagion. Personality and Social Psychology Review, 5, 296–320.

Schaffner, A. D., & Buchanan, L. P. (2010). Evidence-based practices in outpatient treatment for eating disorders. International Journal of Behavioral Consultation and Treatment, 6, 35–44.

Schaffner, A.D. & Buchanan, L.P. (2008). Integrating evidence-based treatments with individual needs in an outpatient facility for eating disorders. Eating Disorders: Journal of Treatment and Prevention, 16(5), 378-392.

Schnitker S. A., & Emmons R. A. (2013). Hegel's thesis–antithesis–synthesis model. In A. L. C. & L. Oviedo (Eds.), Encyclopedia of sciences and religions (pp. 978–978). New York, NY: Springer.

Sedler, M. J. (1983). Freud's concept of working through. Psychoanalytic Quarterly, 52(1), 73–98.

Siegel, D. (2011). Mindsight: The new science of personal transformation. New York, NY: Bantam.

Sims, H. P., & Lorenzi, P. (1992). The new leadership paradigm: Social learning and cognition in organizations. New York, NY: Sage.

Smink. F. E., van Hoeken, D., & Hoek, H. W. (2012). Epidemiology of eating disorders: Incidence, prevalence and mortality rates. Current Psychiatry Reports, 14, 406–414.

Sobell, L., & Sobell, M. (2008). Motivational interviewing strategies and techniques. Retrieved from http://www.nova.edu/gsc/forms/mi_rationale_techniques.pdf.

Solomon, M.A,. (1974). Resistance in family therapy: Some conceptual and technical considerations. The Family Coordinator, 23, 159–163.

St. Clair, M. (2000). Object relations and self psychology: An introduction. Independence, KY: Brooks/Cole.

Steiger, H. (2004). Eating disorders and the serotonin connection: State, trait, and developmental effects. Journal of Psychiatry and Neuroscience, 29, 20–29.

Stephenson, D. (1978). Gestalt therapy primer. Lantham, MD: Jason Aronson.

Summers, R. (1999). Transcending the self: An object relations model of psychoanalytic therapy. Hillsdale, NJ: The Analytic Press.

Teyber, E. (1992). Interpersonal process in psychotherapy: A guide for clinical training. Independence, KY: Brooks/Cole.

Wachtel, P. L. (Ed.). (1982). Resistance: Psychodynamic and behavioral approaches. New York, NY: Plenum Press.

Watzlawick, P., Weakland, C. E., & Fisch, R. (1974). Change: Principles of problem formation and problem resolution. New York, NY: W.W. Norton.

White, M., & Epston, D. (1990). Narrative means to therapeutic ends. New York, NY: Norton.

Willbur, D. (n.d.). Basic needs and parent functions. Retrieved from http://deborahwillbur.com/southerncenter/BasicNeedstable.pdf

Young, J. E., Klosko, J. S., & Weishaar, M. E. (2003). Schema therapy: A practitioner's guide. New York, NY: Guilford Press.

Zeff, T. (2004). The highly sensitive person's survival guide: Essential skills for living well in an overstimulating world (Step-by-Step Guides). New York, NY: New Harbinger.

About the Author

Dr. Linda Buchanan developed her concept of pathological ambivalence while working for more than 30 years with people suffering with eating disorders, a client population in whom ambivalence is not only common but is also potentially fatal if it continues. In 1993, she founded the Atlanta Center for Eating Disorders (ACE), which grew to three locations before she sold the practice to Walden Behavioral Care in 2017. She is now Senior Director of Clinical Services with Walden.

Dr. Buchanan received her PhD from Georgia State University. She received a master's degree from Georgia State University, and a diploma from the Psychological Studies Institute in Christian Counseling, which presented her with the Distinguished Alumnus Award for her work in founding ACE. She is a nationally recognized speaker on the topic of resistance and has published three chapters and several research articles on the treatment of eating disorders. She has been married for more than 30 years and is the mother of two adopted sons.

www.ingramcontent.com/pod-product-compliance
Lightning Source LLC
Chambersburg PA
CBHW022316280326
41932CB00010B/1119